LOS ANGELES
COCKTAILS

An Elegant Collection
of over 100 recipes
Inspired by the City of Angels

KIMBERLY ZERKEL
WITH JOSEPH D. SOLIS

CIDER MILL
PRESS

BOOK
PUBLISHERS

LOS ANGELES COCKTAILS

ISBN-13: 978-1-64643-306-3
ISBN-10: 1-64643-306-8

This book may be ordered by mail from the publisher. Please include $5.99 for postage and handling. Please support your local bookseller first!

Books published by Cider Mill Press Book Publishers are available at special discounts for bulk purchases in the United States by corporations, institutions, and other organizations. For more information, please contact the publisher.

Cider Mill Press Book Publishers
"Where good books are ready for press"
501 Nelson Place
Nashville, TN 37214
cidermillpress.com

Typography: Quiche Sans, Avenir, Copperplate, Sackers, Warnock

Photography credits on page 225

Printed in China

23 24 25 26 27 DSC 5 4 3 2 1

First Edition

CONTENTS

WHO ARE THE

REAL ANGELENOS?

Travel to any metropolitan area and you're bound to overhear an exchange or two about who is truly from there. Those born and raised in a city, regardless of their background, claim authenticity over recent transplants who likely came in search of—or because of—a job.

But anywhere in America, this argument is moot. We know that the original population of any given corner of the country was made up of indigenous peoples. First Nations called this land, their land, home for millennia before today's national and state lines were drawn up. The "real Angelenos," or the first population to live in Los Angeles County, were the Hokan-speaking people, who lived in the Los Angeles basin circa 3000 BCE, followed shortly thereafter by the Tongva and Chumash.

Everyone else, early Spanish missionaries included, is new.

When discussing cocktails, why should population matter? Can the same principle of terroir—the notion that helps us understand that Champagne is made by a group of experts living in one specific region in France, for example—be applied to LA's martinis and Mai Tais? With a city like Los Angeles, it's not about terroir or regionality. It's about how the diverse sights, sounds, and flavors that define the city's cocktail scene arrived there in the first place.

Fast-forward through history and you'll find a city that is marked by people in transit. There is the regular come and go of any inhabited place, of course. LA families pack up and move out, only to be replaced by another unit eager to buy their now million-dollar home. Kids grow up and go off to college, while others anxiously await their acceptance letters from schools like UCLA or University of Southern California.

Like any major international city, Los Angeles is a destination for people from all over the world. Hailing from nearly every continent, as well as from further afield in the United States, individuals move to LA to be close to family, to find work, or to simply enjoy California's coast and sunshine. By 2010, close to 40 percent of Angelenos claimed to be "foreign-born."

Large cities have always had the ability to attract new people from all over the globe. Unlike other metropoles, however, so many newcomers arrive in Los Angeles in search of the one thing that they truly can't find elsewhere: stardom.

Hollywood will always be the ultimate destination for anyone seeking the limelight, whether as an actor, director, writer, dancer, musician, or a bartender looking to put their unique spin on spirits. The stories of a twenty-something packing up their car and driving to LA to "make it" are common enough to be the plotline in countless novels, films, and television shows. But so are the tales of successful Broadway actors who move to California to try out the silver screen, or the international director who's conquered Cannes and now wants to go to the Oscars. They recognize what everyone in Hollywood knows to be true: the entertainment industry is everywhere. True celebrity can only be found in one city in the world.

This is accurate for the music industry as well. Rock bands might start by playing dive bars across the United States, but, as the band Weezer sings, "Beverly Hills/That's where I want to be." Performing at the Hollywood Bowl, trashing luxury hotel rooms, or partying at the Viper Room have been milestones that endless rock 'n' roll bands have aspired to for decades now. Pop artists have joined their ranks, many hoping to occupy as much space on the silver screen as on stage. Rap and hip-hop began in LA as early as the late 1970s, and over the years, as both genres grew in popularity, the city was the birthplace of West Coast rap royalty. LA even draws a hefty number of country singers, much to Nashville's chagrin. "Hello, LA, bye-bye Birmingham," Nancy Sinatra crooned in the 1960s. Thirty years later, Missouri native Sheryl Crow twanged, "All I want to do is have some fun/Until the sun comes up over Santa Monica Boulevard."

Certain new arrivals are lucky enough to quickly see life inside a recording booth, at the head of a boardroom, or on the other side of a production studio's gates. They also get to turn heads as they walk into trendy restaurants, cocktail lounges, or rooftop bars to have a meeting with this executive or that producer.

But quite often, those who arrived in the City of Angels looking for celebrity status will be behind the bar, mixing drinks to pay the bills as they wait for their next big break. Many find their passion in LA's flourishing hospitality scene (which, since 2019, finally boasts several Michelin-star locations).

Opposite LA's mixologists, seated on barstools, are even more hopefuls dressed to the nines and looking to get noticed. They're sipping on cocktails that were invented in LA, like the Moscow Mule, or enjoying a drink built around tequila or rice wine, influenced by the many nationalities and cultures that call this place home.

Every city has a meeting place where things happen. Early twentieth-century Paris had cafés where writers and painters would regularly congregate to write, draw, or debate. Mid-century New York had coffee shops where beatnik poets and folk singers met for performance art. Los Angeles has restaurants and bars where contracts are signed, plots are scribbled onto napkins, and stars are born.

All while gathered around a chilled cocktail, the glass sweating in the Southern California heat.

A BRIEF HISTORY
OF ALCOHOL IN LA

It is ironic that alcohol arrived in the Los Angeles basin at the same time as Christianity. The city would one day become a strategic location on the Prohibition map as the war between born-again teetotalers and everyday lushes raged on. But religious zeal and an intoxicating buzz were introduced to Southern California at the same time with the arrival of the Spanish.

The Tongva, sometimes called the Gabrielino or Gabrieleño, did not produce or drink any alcohol of their own. Their first taste was of Spanish wine, brought by missionaries primarily for ceremonies and other religious purposes. In 1778, the first Californian wines were produced (using Spanish grapes). The missionaries then created their own hybrid—Mission grapes.

Shortly thereafter, Los Angeles' first craft beverage was created. Angelica was wine made from Mission grapes, then mixed with sugar,

resulting in a sherry-like concoction. Like all wines, Angelica was likely used for both pious and pleasurable reasons.

In 1821, following the Mexican War of Independence, Los Angeles was no longer Spanish but Mexican. The newly independent Mexico welcomed immigrants from European countries with a heavy Catholic influence—particularly France. The arrival of Jean-Louis Vignes (a fortuitous name—vignes is French for "grapevines") introduced Los Angeles to French wine and Bordeaux grapes. By 1831, he had founded the El Aliso winery, near the present-day Union Station, California's first winery with no religious affiliation.

Mexican control over Los Angeles was cut short by the Mexican-American War. In 1848, California was purchased by the United States government as part of the Treaty of Guadalupe Hidalgo. Is it any surprise that beer arrived in the City of Angels shortly thereafter? This shift in drinking habits was primarily due to newly arrived German immigrants. Only a few years in as an "American city," and the first downtown LA brewery opened under the odd name of The New York Brewery.

More breweries and saloons popped up around downtown Los Angeles shortly thereafter. By 1879, the Los Angeles Brewing Company opened. The brewery would go on to survive Prohibition and be acquired by Pabst in the 1950s. In true downtown style, the building was shut down and boarded up by the 1980s only to be reborn in the twenty-first century as luxury lofts and artists' studios.

Bars where Angelenos could sip the harder stuff appeared in the late nineteenth century as well. Whiskey, rum, and brandy were staples in the United States throughout the 1800s and into the early 1900s—so much so that it was common for Americans to have a whiskey first thing in the morning. Thanks to Los Angeles' diverse population, other spirits like baijiu from China or tequila from Mexico likely could have been found and enjoyed. But wine, not beer and not spirits, remained king in Los Angeles.

PROHIBITION

On January 17, 1920, when the United States government passed the 18th amendment and Prohibition went into effect—banning production, sales, and consumption of alcohol across the country—LA's gutters ran red with wine. The *Los Angeles Times* reported that the North Cucamonga Winery on Alameda Street alone dumped 35,000 gallons of wine into city sewers that day. The result? Devastation to LA's economy, a corrupt city government, organized crime, and, still, very little sobriety.

The wine flowing through the sewers proved to be an omen. Alcohol would remain present, but it would flow underground. Some wineries and breweries continued to operate by producing tonics or "near beer." Wine-making kits were sold. A clandestine economy formed that specialized in smuggling liquor from Mexico or Canada by way of the Pacific coastline. The alcohol would make its way downtown and then on to the rest of the United States after passing through miles upon miles of tunnels.

It wasn't just sales and transport that moved underground. This was the Roaring Twenties, after all. Parties roared on in secret clubs and speakeasies. The gatherings in locations like King Eddy Saloon, the Del Monte, or the Townhouse in Venice were so epic that generations of bar owners have tried to recreate speakeasies well after Prohibition ended.

The 18th amendment was reversed on December 5, 1933, allowing Americans living through the Depression and on the brink of a second world war to finally have a good, stiff drink legally. Throughout this bleak historical period, many turned to bars and clubs for escapism—and not just through boozy libations.

HOLLYWOOD GLITZ AND GLAMOUR

The Golden Age of Hollywood was already well underway by the time Prohibition had come to an end. Going out for cocktails in Los Angeles—whether in an underground bar or in a newly opened lounge— was just as much about rubbing shoulders with celebrities as it was about enjoying a drink.

Creating a list of the legendary bars from this era is a dizzying task, especially when trying to decide where to start. But The Musso & Frank Grill, established in 1919, has a history as starry as Hollywood itself. Known for its cuisine as well as the famous martini, the location quickly drew a glitzy crowd—as well as a public eager to be seen in their ranks. Although sitting next to Hollywood stars wasn't possible for the everyday Angeleno. Musso & Frank was known for its Back Room, which was guarded by attentive staff who strived to give celebrities privacy to party in peace. From the likes of Charlie Chaplin to Greta Garbo, Groucho Marx, and Marilyn Monroe,

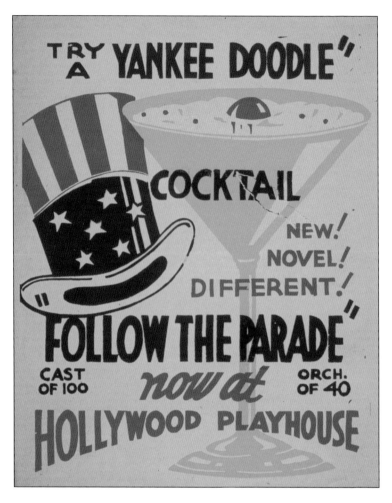

Musso & Frank was (and continues to be) an establishment beloved by the Hollywood elite.

The spot attracted literary royalty as well. F. Scott Fitzgerald, William Faulkner, and T.S. Eliot are just some of the writers who sipped, wrote, and edited in the legendary Back Room. Raymond Chandler was a regular and is said to have written chapters of *The Big Sleep*—a quintessential LA novel—in one of Musso & Frank's booths.

The writers and stars would often be flanked by execs, eager to make deals on the restaurant's pay phone (the first one installed in Hollywood). Then they'd get cozied up in the famous leather banquettes, be waited upon by waiters in red jackets and bowties, and dine on duck and lamb while sipping martinis—all of which you can still experience today.

Another legendary location is The Frolic Room on Hollywood Boulevard. What had originally operated as a speakeasy in 1930 was transformed into a celebrity-bedecked pleasure den. Howard Hughes purchased the neighboring Pantages Theater in 1949, which then went on to host the Academy Awards for five years. The Frolic Room hosted lively after-parties and became a regular watering hole for Frank Sinatra and Judy Garland, as well as the writer Charles Bukowski (whose poetry is read in the bar every evening). Despite its cheerful name, The Frolic Room has a dark side: Elizabeth Short, the Black Dahlia, was last seen alive there before her 1947 murder.

Tourists, regulars, and even the occasional celebrity still stop by The Frolic Room for beers, shots, and other no-fuss drinks. They're welcomed by a talented bar staff, red vinyl barstools, and movie caricatures on the wall (including a mural starring both Albert Einstein and Marilyn Monroe).

To drink like John Wayne or crane your neck to see Cary Grant's reserved booth, you'd have to make your way to Tom Bergin's Horseshoe Tavern & Thoroughbred Club. Bergin's opened in 1936 on Wilshire Boulevard and is now home to the Los Angeles County Museum of Art. It became famous for its Irish Coffee, a mixture of sugar, whiskey, coffee, and Irish cream. The establishment was also beloved for its warm, pub-like interior and ceiling covered in paper shamrocks bearing the names of regulars. Bergin's has since moved to Fairfax, but is still beloved for its caffeinated and boozy signature concoction.

When back rooms and reserved booths simply weren't enough, Hollywood elite would (and still) flock to hotels for ultimate indulgence. The first was the Beverly Hills Hotel, the "Pink Palace" built in 1912 that is well known for its gorgeous grounds and the gorgeous people who stroll them on their way to a private bungalow or to the Polo Lounge for a drink. The 1930s and 1940s are referred to as its "Glamour Years," when Fred Astaire and Carole Lombard were regulars. The hotel was home to Howard Hughes for thirty years after he purchased several bungalows on the property; eager to please their famous client, the hotel staff would follow Hughes's strange instructions to the letter, including delivering his room service order to a specific nook in a specific tree. By the 1960s, the Beatles were sneaking in for dips in the pool and John Lennon was booking a bungalow for privacy with his new love, Yoko Ono. In cocktail history, the Polo Lounge is famous for epic, night-long drinking sessions with Frank Sinatra, Dean Martin, and other members of the Rat Pack. Famous cocktails include The Howard Huges, named after its most eccentric guest, as well as the Moscow Mule and Mai Tai.

The Hollywood Roosevelt Hotel, built in 1927 and named after President Theodore Roosevelt, was more than just an escape for the city's rich and famous. It hosted the first ever Academy Awards ceremony in 1929. Its restaurants and bars are as much for meetings and business brokers as they are for rollicking. But it's famous for its regular clientele, including Marilyn Monroe, who lived there for two years early on in her career. Carole Lombard and Clark Gable were such regulars that the hotel now has the Gable-Lombard Penthouse named after them (the couple paid $5 a night for the 3,200-square-foot room with views of the Hollywood Hills). For cocktails, there are numerous bars to try but perhaps the most famous are the Spare Room and Tropicana Bar, which overlooks the hotel's pool. Celebrities (some who purportedly have keys for discreet, backdoor entry to the bar) still slip in for a drink—a Trop Old Fashioned or Rosy Margarita being favorites.

Further afield on Sunset Boulevard is the Chateau Marmont, and its famed Bar Marmont, which still attracts A-list celebrities today. Built to resemble a castle in France's Loire Valley, the hotel opened in 1929 and attracted stars from the Golden Age of Hollywood almost immediately. Howard Hughes, in search of new faces and new delights, would rent out a room overlooking the pool to spy on bathers below. James Dean, while auditioning for *Rebel Without a Cause*, allegedly jumped out of a window to get the auditioners' attention.

Because of a strict ban on paparazzi, stars have been able to let their hair down a little more than usual at the locale. This is perhaps why Chateau Marmont has become both famed and notorious for celebrity bad behavior. Robin Williams and Robert De Niro partied alongside John Belushi in a bungalow only hours before he died of an overdose there. Lindsey Lohan is forever banned from the premises after racking up a room service bill in the tens of thousands of dollars. Bar Marmont serves a number of classic cocktails—who you get to sip them with is entirely up to you.

INVENTED IN LA:
THE MOSCOW MULE

The Moscow Mule was invented in 1941 at the Cock 'n' Bull restaurant on Sunset Boulevard. It was the result of three entrepreneurs crossing paths. Sophie Berezinski, a Russian immigrant, arrived in Los Angeles with 2,000 copper mugs. She met up with John Martin, who had just purchased the Smirnoff Vodka company, and Jack Morgan, owner of the Cock 'n' Bull, who had begun producing ginger beer. The three, struggling but eager to sell their goods, joined forces—and the rest is history.

TIKI CULTURE

Los Angeles cocktail bars and restaurants were not only known by their celebrity clientele, but for their own touch of Hollywood escapism. From interior design to entertainment to the drinks themselves, many establishments specialized in a curated experience that would stand out, attract attention, and provide guests with a healthy dose of the exotic.

Tiki bars are the prime example. Tiki culture was born in Hollywood in 1933 at a bar and restaurant that was first called Don's Beachcomber before being changed to Don the Beachcomber. The establishment was "Polynesian-themed," and consisted of trappings that owner Raymond Beaumont-Gannt (who would later change his name to Donn Beach) collected while he and his father sailed throughout the South Pacific, rum-running.

Like most tiki bars that would soon follow in Los Angeles and across the United States, Don the Beachcomber was a mishmash of Asian and Pacific Islander cultures and stereotypes. The restaurant sold cocktails and punch spiked with Caribbean rum alongside Cantonese cuisine in a setting filled with a blend of Polynesian décor—masks, tiki torches, rattan, wicker, and flower leis—whose use and symbolism was often romanticized. White Angelenos, hungry (and thirsty) for a taste of the "foreign," flocked to these themed restaurants. Asian Americans and Pacific Islanders often made up the entire waitstaff, regardless of their origin.

What's ironic is that tiki bars are an American creation. And it's not by chance that tiki culture started in the epicenter of show business. After Prohibition, the Great Depression, and two world wars, Hollywood was more than happy to fan the flames of fantasy and escape with movies that portrayed lush scenery, danger, romance, and fascinating locals in a number of South Pacific locations. Tourism to

How Goes It Boys ??

(To be read by men only)

Has the evening been a success? Does she have that mellow look in her eye that you've been hoping for . . . or is she already fumbling for her key so she can dash into her door and make the goodnight shorter . . . (it's been done . . . or did you know?)

Gentlemen, may we make a suggestion . . . . you know, and we know . . . and she knows— that the day of ice cream parlors has passed . . . she's hoping and wondering if there isn't just a remote possibility that you might be thinking of taking her to a sophisticated night spot where there's soft music, smart people and excellent food . . . If that doesn't change the look in her eye, we're sorry we even mentioned it. But, if it does (and we know it will) . . . make a dash for Jerry's Mandalay . . .

BEVERLY HILLS BRANCH OF "JERRY'S JOYNT"

"at the end of the strip"
9236 SUNSET BLVD
BRADSHAW 24553

GEORGE SURPRENANT, JR.

JERRY'S MANDALAY

Featuring

FRANKIE GALLAGHER

•

Dancing to the
Music of
JIMMIE KERR

—4—

Romantic Drama Recreated

●

Recreating Richard Walton Tully's "Bird of Paradise," now playing at the Belasco, Federal Theatres Project is proud to present one of the most successful dramas of the American stage, which had its world premiere in Los Angeles back in 1910 at the old Morosco Theatre. It toured this country and Europe for more than nine years, introducing such outstanding players as Guy Bates Post, Lewis Stone, Laurette Taylor, Lenore Ulric and Bessie Barriscale.

This colorful saga of the South Seas marked the beginning of Hawaiian plays and brought the first band of native musicians to the United States. Out of it has come such productions as "White Cargo," "Congo," "Aloma of the South Seas," and many other intriguing Island dramas. With its music, romance and tragedy set in the tropical surroundings of Hawaii, "Bird of Paradise" is said to be one of the few plays that has lived through the years and retained its original charm for theatregoers.

Story deals with the ill-fated love of Princess Luana, of the Islands, and Dr. Paul Wilson, young American physician, who find themselves hopelessly in love amidst the enchantment of nature's magic spell. How they meet the hazards of racial barriers of the time-worn tradition of "East is East and West is West," is graphically unfolded in three fast-moving acts.

—16—

the Pacific Islands exploded, and the tiki trend blossomed under these conditions. The average American who had to stay home and work could drink in some of the drama at any number of tiki-themed locations—even those in their own backyard or basement.

It is now widely recognized that tiki culture is an example of appropriation. "Polynesian-themed" was an umbrella term for Polynesian, Micronesian, Melanesian, New Zealand, Caribbean, Hawaiian, and even Chinese cultural elements. The name "tiki" is from the Māori name for the first-ever human. Tiki, the man, often appears in the form of a pendant, and such pendants were bought up by American and European tourists who designated it to be a "good luck charm." This imagined "mysticism" was then applied to everything from fiery torches to tribal masks—go-to decorations of any tiki bar.

Strangely enough, tiki cocktails are Caribbean. They likely made their way into tiki culture through an entanglement of sailing stories from the Pacific, and pirating lore from the Caribbean Islands. The most famous tiki cocktail is the Mai Tai, allegedly invented in 1944 at Trader Vic's, a tiki lounge in the San Francisco Bay Area—although Donn Beach claimed the drink was his brainchild. Though many bartenders today add coconut to their Mai Tai, the original included a blend of juices, syrups, and Caribbean rum. Other famous concoctions include the Zombie and the Painkiller, among other colorful names. Tiki cocktails are almost always rum-based and known for their syrupy sweetness.

Tiki culture has evolved over the years. The first wave of change came after World War II, when soldiers returned to the United States after having been exposed to the actual South Pacific. Tiki cocktails have seen a recent revival in Los Angeles and around the country as bartenders are eager to revisit retro recipes and give them their own twist. The appropriation and cultural insensitivities associated with tiki culture continue to be addressed. Those who hope to revive this slew of cocktails that were born in Los Angeles attempt to do so by focusing on the now-familiar flavors and disassociating themselves from tiki's shadowed past.

Alongside reinvented tiki bars are a growing number of Asian and Pacific Islander–owned bars, lounges, and restaurants that specialize in libations that are a truer testament to each respective culture. Asian and Pacific Islander communities are integral to Los Angeles' identity—close to 11 percent of the city is of Asian or Pacific Islander descent. Having their authentic flavors and customs represented—as opposed to the romanticized and inaccurate stereotypes of the past—is part of what helps LA's cocktail scene thrive today.

INVENTED IN LA:
RAY'S MISTAKE

This popular tiki drink was invented at Tiki Ti and is still served there today. Ray Buhen, the original owner of the bar, went to make a customer an anting, but, as the name would suggest, made a mistake. The customer preferred this new version. After Ray perfected the blend, his mistake became a fan favorite.

FLAVORS OF MEXICO

Los Angeles was a Mexican city before it was an American one. The Pobladores, a group of forty-four settlers and four soldiers, arrived in the basin in 1781. The entire region was part of Mexico until it was purchased by the United States after the Mexican-American War in 1848. To say that Angeleno culture is "influenced" by Mexico is more than just inadequate; it's completely inaccurate. Mexican and LA culture have always been intertwined.

LA is home to the United States' largest Mexican American population. Some say that Greater Los Angeles is the largest Mexican city outside of Mexico and the largest Spanish-speaking city not located in Mexico or Spain. The population is a mixture of families who have been in LA from the beginning, as well as the descendants of workers who arrived before World War II with US-government-sponsored job contracts. A second wave arrived after World War II by way of the bracero, or guest worker, program to address agricultural labor shortages. This program, which could not meet the demand of jobs with ample contracts, is at the heart of continued immigration and political disputes between the United States and Mexico today.

Families arriving from Mexico—and their generations of descendants who have only known Los Angeles as home—have forever defined the city, from politics to neighborhood boundaries, from slang to the flavors that LA's culinary scene is known for. These are all due to the intrinsic link between Mexican and Los Angeles culture. Today, the number of Angelenos of Mexican origin or descent clocks in at 1.91 million—roughly half the entire population. Did some recently emigrate here? Sure. But their presence, culture, language, and impact have always been here.

Despite the popularity of drinks like the margarita, beer or straight tequila are what most Mexicans imbibe on a regular basis.

The origins of both drinks go back all the way to the Aztec empire. Prior to Spanish conquest, the Aztecs drank a corn beer and a fermented drink called pulque, made from the sap of an agave plant (pulque is still consumed today). When the Spanish arrived, European barley-based beer-making was introduced. The Mexican beer industry grew with the arrival of German immigrants in the late 1800s.

The distillation of mezcal started in coastal regions in the sixteenth century. When production arrived in Jalisco in the seventeenth century, a new variant was created: tequila. Tequila is made from blue agave and is named after the town at the foot of the Tequila Volcano. Tequila began to be exported to the United States in 1884.

Mexican beer, mezcal, and tequila were likely as present in Los Angeles as they were in other cities across Mexico in the nineteenth and early twentieth centuries. But the drinks were transformed into the staples they are today during Prohibition. Angelenos traveled across the border into Mexico to party aboveground without the fear of getting caught. Tijuana attracted the wealthiest Californians with the prospect of not only drinking, but gambling.

The invention of the margarita comes from this era. There are multiple stories on the drink's origin. Most are romanticized tales that revolve around Mexican bartenders doing their best to impress a beautiful-but-fussy American woman who has arrived on the arm of a wealthy businessman (one such woman credited with inspiring the margarita was Rita Hayworth, whose original name was Margarita Carmen Cansino). The likeliest story, however, is that the Daisy, a popular cocktail with lemon or lime juice as well as gin, brandy, or whiskey, was made for Americans drinking across the border with readily available tequila. The new drink was named margarita, the Spanish word for daisy. Margaritas grew popular in Southern California and other states across the border. The frozen margarita, created

by a Mexican restaurant owner in Dallas, took off in the 1970s and became a Tex-Mex favorite across the country.

North of the border throughout Prohibition, Los Angeles' oldest surviving Mexican restaurants often had to disguise themselves as "Spanish" or "Sonoran" to attract white customers who otherwise held racist views of their fellow Angelenos and their culture. This began to evolve ever so slightly in the 1950s, when eating out and drinking in Mexican cantina-style restaurants grew in popularity (although the adjectives "Spanish," "Sonoran," and "Mexican" were still used almost interchangeably).

The oldest surviving Mexican restaurants in Greater Los Angeles today are El Cholo, which opened in 1927, La Golondrina Mexican Cafe, opened in 1928, and El Coyote, opened in 1931. The latter is both famous and infamous—it's where Sharon Tate dined before being murdered by the Manson family hours later (and was thus featured in Quentin Tarentino's *Once Upon a Time in Hollywood*).

Today, everything from laid-back taco trucks to Instagram-ready bespoke cocktail bars prevail, serving up variations of the margarita, as well as palomas, batangas, micheladas, and more. Other cocktails that some Americans incorrectly associate with Mexico—piña coladas and daiquiris, for example—are Caribbean, although new variations that substitute rum with tequila now exist.

DIVE BARS AND HAIR METAL OF THE 1980S

The music industry's impact on LA culture is as important as Hollywood's. Los Angeles is, after all, a music city. Capitol Records is perhaps the most notable landmark that pays tribute to this. But countless other recording studios exist and have been attracting talent since the 1930s.

LA remains at the center of all things rock 'n' roll, as well as rap and hip-hop. But its zenith moment was in the 1980s, when having big hair, flashy makeup, and androgynous clothing made of spandex or leather were just as important as playing the guitar. Whether you call it glam rock or hair metal, there are many names given to this particular era and sound. But it's when rock stars were royalty and held court at bars up and down West Hollywood's Sunset Strip.

In 1981, a new band called Mötley Crüe played a show at a nightclub called The Starwood, south of Sunset Strip on Santa Monica Boulevard. The Starwood had originally been a jazz nightclub in the 1960s. Over time, the location began to host gigs for early punk and metal bands. But the success of Mötley Crüe's single performance signaled the beginning of the glam rock era. Nearby bars and clubs began booking similar shows. The Starwood closed two months later, but its owner, Elmer Valentine, had already opened up other venues along the strip.

Famous locations included The Roxy Theater, known as The Roxy, where the infamous madame to the stars Heidi Fleiss threw exclusive and over-the-top parties for rockers. Whisky a Go Go, a former go-go club from the 1960s and 1970s, switched over to metal in the mid-1980s and became one of Sunset Strip's top spots.

The Rainbow Bar and Grill was a popular spot to go and guzzle drinks between sets. It was common to see both bands and fans crowded into the same spot to imbibe before and after shows while planning their next stop for the evening. By 1986, partygoers—who were on the Strip whether it was Friday night or Tuesday—would finish up the evening at The Cathouse, a club that featured DJs spinning rock records. The Cathouse was considered the "epicenter" of glam rock decadence and was home to outrageous parties with bands like Guns n' Roses, LA Guns, and Jet Boy. The nostalgia that exists around The Cathouse has resulted in multiple attempts to reopen and rebrand throughout the years.

What was the Sunset Strip crowd consuming, besides tons of hair-spray? Like any good dive dweller, the most sought-after combination for this crowd was usually a shot and a beer. Well whiskey was the most popular liquor, and slapdash cocktails like a whiskey and coke or a whiskey ginger were staples.

Glam rock gave way to 1990s' grunge. Though dive bars continued to be great spots to hear live music, the eccentric hedonism of hair metal was replaced by a moodier vibe. The Rainbow Grills and Cat-houses were replaced by fern bars and Europe-inspired, techno-spin-ning nightclubs. A shot and beer was "upgraded" to the more complicated Appletini and Cosmo of the late 1990s and early 2000s.

LOS ANGELES COCKTAILS TODAY

Gone are the days of every bartender and mixologist biding their time behind a bar while waiting for a big break on the silver screen. Los Angeles' hospitality scene is thriving, and some of the city's most cre-ative types express themselves through their recipes.

These artists have helped define LA's current cocktail culture, but they remain the newest members. The Los Angeles cocktail scene is like the city itself—historic, layered, and indefinable. LA cannot be defined by one thing. Its very landscape is a mixture of city, suburbs, mountain, and ocean. Its population has always been diverse, cosmopolitan, and polylingual. Its cocktail menu is as diverse and includes old classics, like Martinis and Old Fashioneds, that can be imbibed by tourists and locals alike at old Hollywood haunts. It also features the latest generation of tiki cocktails that pays homage to traditional tiki flavors while transforming tiki culture into something completely new. Then there are the latest speakeasies, a nod to the difficult-yet-rollicking Prohibition era. Then there are the bars that specialize in tequila- and mezcal-based drinks, an homage to Los Angeles' Mexican heritage, as well as corner joints that carry a bottle of both because they're staples. At the end, there are the beers and shots of LA's dive bar scene being enjoyed by locals as well as bartenders just finishing their shifts.

It's this intricate blend of flavors and locations that adds to the city's richness. The beauty of LA has always been in its complexity—the kind of complexity you find in a perfectly mixed drink.

BAR KEEPER'S
GUIDE TO

SETTING UP AN
LA HOME BAR

The home bar is not a new concept by any stretch. But in 2006, as the ripple effects from craft cocktail and mixology movements began to make it into people's homes, Bar Keeper became the go-to destination for Angelenos looking to add depth to their home bars. This was due to the dedicated staff's extensive knowledge of bar tools, small-batch spirits, and glassware.

When the COVID-19 pandemic shut the world down, Bar Keeper also became one of the only ways to get a decent cocktail in town. Sure, you could order a cocktail to go or pick up something premade at a local liquor store, but how would you get your Mezcal Negroni fix or the Gin Martini made with your favorite gin and vermouth combo on a Tuesday afternoon? The store found itself an essential business during 2020. "We weren't saving lives, but if you're going to drink, why not do it right?" says Lonnie Finley. "We had an uptick in customers stocking up on bar tools, spirits, amaros, bitters, and items generally purchased by the bartender or super cocktail enthusiast."

So, here is Bar Keeper's expert advice for stocking your home bar so you can make top-shelf drinks in the comfort of your own home, no matter the circumstances.

GLASSWARE

Coupe and/or Nick and
  Nora
Rocks glass and double
  rocks glass, aka old-
  fashioned and double
  old-fashioned
Collins glass
Gin and tonic glass
Tiki mug or tiki glass
Cordial glass
Vintage set (for the friends
  you trust)

TOOLS

Bar spoon, weighted with
  muddler
Jigger, Japanese or
  Leopold
Mixing glass
Boston shaker (18 oz./28
  oz.)
Strainers, Hawthorne and
  julep
Mesh strainer
Peeler
Zester
Paring knife
Muddler
Ice cube tray for large and
  Collins rocks
Fast-flow pourers and
  caps
Citrus squeezers
Bar mat
Bar towels
Cocktail picks

SPIRITS

GIN

A London Dry
Mahon
Future
Gwendolyn
Common Ground Black
   Currant Tyme
Roku
Fred Jerbis 43

St. George (Botanivore,
   Terroir)
Moletto
Four Pillars Olive
Barr Hill Tom Cat Barrel
   Aged
Rally

VODKA

Loft and Bear
Hera the Dog
Nat Kidder

Black Cow
Amass

TEQUILA

Tequila Ocho
Fortaleza
La Gritona

Lalo
Tessoro Number 5 Blanco/
   Repsado

MEZCAL

San Bartolo Mezcal
　　Valentin Lopez Espadín
El Mero Mero Espadín
Verde Memento

Yuu Baal Espadín
Mayalen Machetazo
　　Espadín

RUM

Smith & Cross
Doctor Bird Jamaican Rum
Coruba Dark Jamaican
　　Rum

Plantation Rum (O.F.T.D.
　　Overproof 69 &
　　Pineapple)
Saison Rum Pale

RYE, BOURBON, WHISKEY –

Old Overholt Bonded
　　Straight Rye
Uncle Nearest 1856
Home Base Bourbon
Pinhook Rye (BK Selection)
Rare Character Bourbon
　　(BK Selection)
James E. Pepper Rye

Barrell Seagrass Rye
Lost Irish Irish Whiskey
Redwood Empire Pipe
　　Dream Bourbon & Lost
　　Monarch Straight
　　Whiskey
Old 49 California Whiskey

JAPANESE WHISKY

Nikka Days

Suntory Toki

MODIFIERS

St. George Absinthe

Mario's Hard Espresso

Taylor's Velvet Falernum

Green and Yellow
   Chartreuse

Lillet Blanc

Suze

Amaro Montenegro

Amaro Nonino

Cynar

Forthave Spirits Red
   Apertivo

Leopold Bros. Aperitivo

Amaro Angeleno

Alma Tepec Chile Liqueur

Greenbar Distillery
   liqueurs

Miracle Mile Bitters

Angostura Bitters

MiddleBar Small Batch
   Bloody Mary Mix

Girl Walks into a Bar
   Margarita Mix

Fever-Tree Tonic

Lo-Fi Aperitifs vermouth

Bordiga vermouths

Foro Vermouth

Carpano Antica

GARNISHES

The Cocktail Garnish

Maraschino cherries

MiddleBar Bourbon
   Cherries

PICANTE AMOR

This cocktail is inspired by the SoCal love for agave spirits, tiki, and making everything ourselves. The idea was to take the popular spicy margarita and make it tiki. This is a drier style of tiki drink. The addition of mezcal gives a smoky undertone, fortified by the smoke from chipotle bitters.

GLASSWARE: Tiki glass

GARNISH: Pineapple frond, lime wedge

- 1½ oz. Casa Rica Reposado (or other oaky, not too sweet reposado)
- ¼ oz. La Luna Cupreata Mezcal
- ½ oz. falernum (they make their own; Lucky Falernum works)
- 1½ oz pineapple juice or 2 oz. fresh lime juice
- ¼ oz. agave syrup (1:1 agave & water)
- 2 dashes chipotle bitters (homemade, or anything smoky or spicy)

1. In a mixing glass, combine all of the ingredients and shake.

2. Strain the cocktail over fresh ice into a tiki glass.

3. Garnish with a pineapple frond, lime wedge, fun straw, and umbrella.

LONNIE'S FAVORITE LA COCKTAIL

BOLITA

FAMILY MEAL

GLASSWARE: Rocks glass, rimmed with Bay Leaf Savory Salt

- 2 oz. Lechon Apple Brandy
- 1½ oz. Cherry Sweet 'n' Sour
- 1 spritz mezcal

1. Rim the rocks glass with the Bay Leaf Savory Salt.

2. Build the cocktail in a cocktail shaker, shake with full-cube ice, and strain over new full-cube ice in the rocks glass.

3. Top with a spritz of mezcal.

LECHON APPLE BRANDY: Combine 160g melted and strained lechon pork fat and 1250ml Laird's Straight Applejack in a container, mix well, cover, and let steep at room temperature for 24 hours. Place the container in the freezer for at least 1 hour. Skim off the solidified fat and strain through a coffee filter. Store in bottles.

BAY LEAF SAVORY SALT: In a spice grinder, combine 4g dried bay leaf (broken up), 4g dried thyme, 8g green peppercorns, and 8g coriander seeds and grind until fine. Sift the ground spices through a chinois to remove the larger pieces, and regrind the larger pieces. Repeat 3 to 4 times. Add the finely ground spices to a bowl, being sure to scrape out the residue on the inside of the grinder. Add 20g smoked paprika, 4g cayenne pepper, 12g citric acid, 12g white sugar, and 260g salt to the bowl with the spice mixture and mix well. Store in a container with a lid.

CHERRY SWEET 'N' SOUR: Combine 1064g 100% tart cherry juice, 643g sugar, and 52g malic acid in a container, stir well until sugar has dissolved, and refrigerate.

THE L.A. SPIRITS AWARDS

You're staring at a perplexing array of tequilas on a shelf in your favorite liquor store with no idea which to choose. Then a gold medal on one of the bottles catches your eye, and your decision becomes a lot easier. This is what spirits competitions are all about: the medals that spirits brands win at reputable competitions testify to a spirit's quality, and distilleries all over the globe hope to earn competition medals that can help them attract new customers and sell more of their products. But who are the judges bestowing these awards, and which competition's medals can you trust? To instill consumer confidence, it stands to reason that such guidance should come from a team of judges with whom buyers can relate.

When the L.A. Spirits Awards' cofounders Nicolette Teo and Joel Blum launched their new competition in 2019, they sought out a judging panel that would best reflect the contemporary spirits industry, an industry that, like its consumers, has become more culturally and racially diverse, more youthful, more creative, and less predominantly male. Their wildly diverse team is made up of journalists and bloggers, bar owners and mixologists, and spirits educators and influencers, all chosen for the transformative roles they play in the spirits field. And what better place than Los Angeles for this new breed of competition?

Werner Herzog, the German film director, was once asked why he made his home in Los Angeles, and he explained that the city has considerably more substance than it generally receives credit for. The fri-

volity of Hollywood glitz and glamour, he said, "is a very thin crust. Behind it is an enormous intensity of culture and creative energy... that ultimately decides the big things." Los Angeles has long had an outsize influence on taste and culture, and in recent years that influence has extended to spirits and cocktail culture, with a vibrant mixology and bar scene that's grabbing global imaginations. The following recipes reflect that fact, which is why they are favored by the L.A. Spirits Awards team, which includes all of the wonderful folks in the team photograph opposite: bottom row (seated) left to right: Nicolette Teo, cofounder L.A. Spirits Awards; Erick Castro, Hungry Bartender; Samara Davis, Black Bourbon Society; Karla Alindahao, *ForbesLife*; Caroline Pardilla, *Imbibe* magazine; Amie Ward, The Healthtender; second row (standing) left to right: Masahiro Urushido,

Katana Kitten; Mark Stoddard, gin expert; Tim McKirdy, Vinepair; Raul Pool, The Airliner; Tiffanie Barriere, independent bartender and educator; John deBary, bar expert and writer, Clyde Davis, Jr., Team Spirits Imports Company and spirits mentor; Joseph D. Solis, Sol Hospitality Group; Kim Haasarud, Garden Bar PHX and The Cocktail Collaborative; Derek Brown, Positive Damage Inc.; Eryn Reece, Banzabar and Freemans Restaurant; Joel Blum, cofounder L.A. Spirits Awards.

THE VIRAGO

What could be more quintessentially LA than the tiki bar? The culturally confused lounge genre fits the city's character like Mayan Revival motels and Morocco-inspired car washes, enduring in a way that most hat-shaped restaurants and anthropomorphic hot dog stands do not. Its oldest tiki bar, the Tonga Hut, was created in 1958 by brothers Ace and Edwin Libby. Today, there's still some serious mixological magic taking place here.

Beverage director Marie King is a master rum specialist who has brought new life to the tiki cocktail. The Virago, long a pejorative used to describe strong or domineering women, is her contribution to the modern movement to reclaim the word as one of female empowerment. A twist on Donn Beach's Vicious Virgin, it is certainly strong—it's a tiki drink, after all!—but only becomes domineering if you can't handle your liquor.

GLASSWARE: 16 oz. glass or a favorite tiki mug

GARNISH: Edible orchid, orange slice

- 1½ oz. Montaña Oro Rum (moderately aged column-still rum)
- 1 oz. Rhum Clément Select (moderately aged rhum agricole from Martinique)
- ¾ oz. falernum (Tonga Hut makes its own; you may substitute John D. Taylor's Velvet Falernum)
- ½ oz. passion fruit puree
- ½ oz. honey syrup (1:1)
- ¾ oz. fresh lemon juice
- 1 oz. orange juice

1. Combine all of the ingredients in a cocktail shaker and add cracked ice. Shake to agitate and dilute, then pour the cocktail into the glass or mug.

2. Garnish with the orchid and orange slice.

SUPERNOVA LAVA BURST

BROKEN SHAKER

Broken Shaker came to LA to make its mark and quickly made itself at home. One of the nation's four acclaimed Freehand Hotel bars, Broken Shaker's rooftop poolside setting offers sweeping views of the city and a fun, laid-back ambience. But don't let the vibe fool you: this is a serious cocktail bar with a notable cocktail program that is a favorite of the L.A. Spirits Awards team.

The bar's charismatic beverage director, Christine Wiseman, began as a chef, but after craving a change, found herself behind the bar. You can still see her culinary background in her cocktail recipes, each with layers of flavor and components that make those flavors shine. Wiseman started racking up award after award for herself and the establishments she worked at. One sip of the Supernova Lava Burst makes it clear why this is one of the L.A. Spirits Awards' staff favorites.

GLASSWARE: Collins glass
GARNISH: Pineapple crescent, edible flower,
and edible glitter (optional)

- 10 oz. Bombay Sapphire Gin
- ½ oz. Chinola Passion Fruit Liqueur
- ½ oz. Ancho Reyes Verde
- 1 oz. Pineapple Cacao Nib Shrub
- ¾ oz. fresh lemon juice

1. Combine all of the ingredients in a cocktail shaker with ice, shake well, and then strain into the Collins glass over ice.

2. Garnish with the pineapple crescent, edible flower, and, if desired, glitter.

PINEAPPLE CACAO NIB SHRUB: Combine 2 chopped pineapples with the skin still on, 4qts sugar, 4qts rice wine vinegar, 4qts water, and 100g cacao nibs in a pan and bring to a simmer for 15 minutes. Place everything in a container and let sit overnight. Strain the next day into a clean container and refrigerate until needed. Use within 3 weeks.

LOWKEY LUAU

YAEL VENGROFF

ales of the Cocktail Foundation's 2018 Bartender of the Year Yael Vengroff is head of bars and mixology programming for SBE's Katsuya and S Bar concepts. In an interview with *The Tasting Panel Magazine* Vengroff bristled at being called a mixologist, saying "at the end of the day, there are plenty of people who can be mixologists at home—but are they bartenders? The romance is the bar." Ironically, Vengroff doesn't do that much bartending these days since her job keeps her plenty busy developing menus and training staff. But that doesn't mean she can't conjure up a fabulous drink on demand.

- ½ oz. Giffard Banane
- ¾ oz. Branca Menta
- 1½ oz. Ten to One Caribbean Dark Rum
- 3½ oz. matcha colada

1. Combine all of the ingredients in a cocktail shaker with a small amount of crushed ice and shake vigorously, until all of the ice is dissolved.

2. Pour directly into the tiki glass and add more crushed ice.

3. Wrap the banana leaves around the inside of the glass and insert a straw, then use the julep strainer to create a dome on top.

PIÑA DE VICTORIOSO

SOL AGAVE

Sol Agave started out as a taco truck before its metamorphosis into a brick-and-mortar restaurant. Its founders, Jesus Galvez and Chef Manny Velasco, now have several award-winning restaurants, including one in the mammoth L.A. Live entertainment complex, and Sol Agave has equally evolved into a serious source of upscale cocktails. The Piña de Victorioso with Victorioso Espadín, a gold medal–winning mezcal from the 2022 L.A. Spirits Awards, is sublime on its own, but you can't deny that a top-shelf sipping spirit is a fine way to start a cocktail.

GLASSWARE: Tajín-rimmed cocktail glass

GARNISH: Pineapple leaves

- 3 slices roasted pineapple
- 2 oz. Victorioso Espadín Mezcal
- 1 oz. fresh lime juice
- 1 oz. pineapple juice
- 1 slice jalapeño

1. Add the pineapple slices to a cocktail shaker and muddle.

2. Add ice, then the mezcal, lime juice, pineapple juice, and jalapeño. Shake vigorously, then strain into the prepared cocktail glass over ice.

3. Garnish with the pineapple leaves.

CENTRAL

LOS ANGELES

CAMPHOR

FAR BAR

GOOD CLEAN FUN

HERE AND NOW

NICK + STEF'S STEAKHOUSE

OTIUM

GENERAL LEE'S

REDBIRD

GRAND MASTER RECORDS

MUSSO & FRANK

GUELAGUETZA

L os Angeles is a sprawling urban region with many hubs for many different communities. The downtown area and its immediate surroundings have flourished of late, as all of these cocktails make clear.

THE SAINT-GERMAIN

CAMPHOR

Co-executive chefs Max Boonthanakit and Lijo George founded Camphor in early 2022, intending to carve out space for a modern French bistro in Los Angeles cuisine culture. Mission accomplished, considering that the restaurant was awarded a Michelin star in its first year of operation.

In the *Michelin Guide* write-up of Camphor, this cocktail is dubbed "elegant," no doubt a nod to the eponymous 6th arrondissement quarter in Paris known for shopping and that Parisian je ne sais quoi.

GLASSWARE: Water glass
GARNISH: Grated lime zest

- 1½ oz. tequila blanco
- ¾ oz. Yellow Chartreuse
- ½ oz. pineapple gomme
- 1 oz. fresh lime juice
- 2 large sage leaves

1. Combine all of the ingredients in a cocktail shaker with ice, shake well, and strain into the water glass over pebble ice.

2. Garnish with the lime zest.

LE MARAIS

With another nod to a chic neighborhood in Paris, this drink is colored and flavored by the pleasant bitterness of an aperitif made from gentian root.

GLASSWARE: Nick and Nora glass
GARNISH: Expressed lemon twist and skewered marinated strawberry

- 1 oz. Park VS Cognac
- ¾ oz. Buffalo Trace Bourbon
- ½ oz. Tawny Port 10 Year
- ¼ oz. Verjus rojo infused with Harry's Berries
- ¼ oz. gentian aperitif
- ¼ oz. Giffard Banana Liqueur

1. Combine all of the ingredients in a mixing glass with ice and stir until properly chilled and diluted, and then use a julep strainer to pour the cocktail into the Nick and Nora glass.

2. Express the lemon twist over the drink, discard, and garnish with the marinated strawberry.

PAPA LOVES MAMBO

FAR BAR

"A friend, Joanne Martinez, and I were coming up with drinks for a tiki pop-up event and had consumed quite a bit of Don Papa Daiquiris just to get our creative juices flowing and I decided to make a passion fruit daiquiri; the rum and Chinola paired so well together, it was a match made in heaven. So aromatic and sweet but tart, and that oaky vanilla from the Don Papa—it was perfect. Then suddenly 'Papa Loves Mambo' starts playing and I just had to name it that"—Jesse Sepulveda

GLASSWARE: Chilled coupe
GARNISH: Edible orchid

- 1½ oz. Don Papa Small Batch Rum
- ¾ oz. Chinola Passion Fruit Liqueur
- 1 oz. fresh lime juice
- ¼ oz. simple syrup

1. Combine all of the ingredients in a cocktail shaker with ice, shake well, and double strain into the chilled coupe.

2. Garnish with the orchid.

XXXTRA DIRTY MARTINI

GOOD CLEAN FUN

Ari Stevens's natural wine shop and seasons-inspired restaurant applies the same organic and all-natural standards to its excellent and surprising cocktail program. The elegant simplicity is tasted, like in this martini riff.

GLASSWARE: Cocktail glass
GARNISH: 2 cocktail olives

- 1½ oz. shochu
- 1 oz. dry vermouth
- ½ oz. olive brine

1. Combine all of the ingredients in a cocktail shaker with ice, stir, and strain into the cocktail glass.

2. Garnish with 2 of your favorite cocktail olives.

FIRE OF THE DRAGON NEGRONI SBAGLIATO

GOOD CLEAN FUN

Traditionally, a Negroni is made with Campari, sweet vermouth, and gin, while a Negroni Sbagliato, or a "broken" Negroni, uses sparkling wine instead of gin. In this Ari Stevens creation, the barley shochu is "broken," but you won't want to fix it once you taste it.

GLASSWARE: Rocks glass
GARNISH: Dried citrus wheel

- 1½ oz. sweet vermouth
- 1½ oz. barley shochu
- 1½ oz. Prosecco

1. Combine the vermouth and shochu in a cocktail shaker with ice, stir, and strain into the rocks glass over ice.

2. Top with the Prosecco and garnish with the dried citrus wheel.

FROZEN PORNSTAR MARTINI

HERE AND NOW

Inspired by the original Pornstar Martini that was created by Douglas Ankrah in London in 2002, we gave this an LA twist as a frozen drink. At the bar, the drink is batched in a frozen drink machine, but this home bar–friendly recipe makes a single serving in a blender.

GLASSWARE: Collins glass

- 1½ oz. vodka
- ½ oz. Chinola Passion Fruit Liqueur
- ¼ oz. Licor 43
- 2 oz. Frozen Passion Fruit Syrup
- ½ oz. fresh lime juice

1. Combine all of the ingredients in a blender, process until smooth, and serve.

FROZEN PASSION FRUIT SYRUP: Blend 1 part passion fruit puree with 2 parts simple syrup, pour the mixture into ice cube trays, and freeze.

"OH, WHAT'S THAT?"

HERE AND NOW

With a coupe that looks a teacup, guests are always asking, "Oh what's that?" So we aptly renamed our espresso martini "Oh, What's That?"

GLASSWARE: Coupe

GARNISH: 3 espresso beans

- 2 oz. Argonaut Saloon Strength Brandy
- 1 oz. brewed espresso
- ½ oz. Mr. Black Coffee Liqueur
- ½ oz. simple syrup

1. Combine all of the ingredients in a cocktail shaker with ice, shake well, and double strain into the coupe.

2. Garnish with the 3 espresso beans.

NICK + STEF'S STEAKHOUSE

Located at the Wells Fargo Center in downtown Los Angeles, Nick + Stef's Steakhouse is an award-winning and top-rated steak restaurant founded by chef Joachim Splichal and named after his twins. The cocktail menu, put together by sommelier Marlon Dominguez, prides itself on exotic and elite ingredients fit for a steakhouse atmosphere.

LA MUJEN

NICK + STEF'S STEAKHOUSE

Marlon Dominguez calls La Mujen "our version of a daiquiri," and its ingredients work together to "add a savory note to the already rich and full-bodied shochu."

GLASSWARE: Coupe

- 1 Luxardo maraschino cherry
- 1½ oz. Mujen X 10 Year Shochu
- ½ oz. Luxardo Maraschino Liqueur
- 1 oz. fresh lime juice
- ½ oz. pineapple juice

1. Place the cherry in the coupe and set it aside.

2. Combine all of the ingredients in a cocktail shaker with ice, shake well for 15 seconds, and strain into the coupe.

THE BATTLE

NICK + STEF'S STEAKHOUSE

This drink takes its name from the Battle of Puebla during the Franco-Mexican War, setting its main spirit from Mexico against two French liqueurs and resulting in an explosion of flavors.

GLASSWARE: Coupe

GARNISH: Brandied cherry

- ¾ oz. Gracias a Dios Gin
- ¾ oz. Suze
- ¾ oz. Yellow Chartreuse
- ¾ oz. fresh lemon juice

1. Combine all of the ingredients in a cocktail shaker with ice, shake well for 15 seconds, and strain into the coupe.

2. Garnish with the brandied cherry.

TEA & HONEY

Marlon Dominguez crafted this light and refreshing sour as a dinner complement to help cut through the richness of Nick + Stef's dry-aged steaks.

GLASSWARE: Sour glass

- **2 oz. Chamomile-Infused Hangar 1 Vodka**
- **½ oz. honey**
- **½ oz. simple syrup**
- **1 oz. fresh lemon juice**
- **1 egg white**
- **2 dashes Angostura Bitters**

1. Combine all of the ingredients, except the bitters, in a cocktail shaker with ice, shake well for 15 seconds, strain into the sour glass, and add the bitters.

CHAMOMILE-INFUSED HANGAR 1 VODKA: Add 5 tbsps. loose chamomile tea to a bottle of Hangar 1 Vodka and steep for 2 hours. Strain and filter the vodka into a rubber-top decanter to store.

OTIUM

Named after a Latin word that describes a place designated for lei-surely social gatherings, Otium's cocktails reflect chef Timothy Hollingsworth's "elegant rusticity."

WHAT'S UP DOC?

OTIUM

As the restaurant at the Broad Museum, Otium's offerings possess a playful artistic swagger, like this veg-centric cocktail.

GLASSWARE: Chilled coupe

GARNISH: Petite carrot

- 1½ oz. The Botanist Islay Dry Gin
- ½ oz. Aperol
- ¼ oz. Clement Mahina Coconut Liqueur
- ¾ oz. fresh lemon juice
- 1 oz. carrot juice
- 1 oz. Coconut Cream
- 2 dashes Scrappy's Cardamom Bitters

1. Combine all of the ingredients in a cocktail shaker with ice, shake well, and double strain into the chilled coupe.

2. Garnish with the carrot.

COCONUT CREAM: Combine equal parts coconut milk and granulated sugar and mix well.

OTIUM

OTIUM

Leaning into Japanese flavors, this beautifully balanced creation is a smoky-sweet sipper that makes you slow down, think, and appreciate. No wonder it's named after the place.

GLASSWARE: Double Old Fashioned glass

GARNISH: Green tea–washed ginger candy

- 1½ oz. Hibiki Harmony Whisky
- ¼ oz. Suntory Toki Whisky
- ¼ oz. L'orgeat Almond Liqueur
- ¾ oz. fresh lemon juice
- ½ oz. honey syrup (3:1)
- 1 bar spoon yuzu juice extract
- 2 dashes Miracle Mile Yuzu Bitters

1. Combine all of the ingredients in a cocktail shaker with ice, shake well, and double strain into the double Old Fashioned glass over one large ice cube.

2. Garnish with the green tea–washed ginger candy.

GENERAL LEE'S

Describing itself as having "ancient culture, classic style, contemporary seasoning," General Lee's has roots in the old-school traditions of Chinese American restaurants, but today it's all about bold drinks and killer music with a retro-red vibe. Look for a single red bench in an alley to find the door, and, if you want to avoid the crowd, come early.

LITTLE ROSE

One day, Mai-Qwai (Little Rose) ran home angry to her mother saying, "Mü-Tsing, I do not want my name to be Rose any longer. I was in Dun-Qure's garden just now, and she asked me, 'Which flower do you like best of all in our garden?' and I said I liked my name-flower best. Then they all laughed and said, 'We do not. Do you not see the thorns on the roses? When we pass near we tear our dresses. When we touch them the blood flows from our hands. No, we do not like the roses. The baby cow does not like them either. They stick her nose when she tries to eat, and even mother cannot pick them without scissors. Once when she had a large bunch of roses, little sister tried to get one and it stuck her hands and face so that she cried many hours. Other flowers do not make trouble like that, and we do not see why anyone likes the rose best. We think it very foolish to like a trouble flower and be named for it.' I do not like my name-flower any more, Mü-Tsing, and I do not want to bear its name."

"Do not cry, dear child," said her mother. "I will tell you some things about the rose. Do you like rose sugar?"

"Yes, very much," Rose answered, her face growing bright.

"And rose oil?"

"Oh, yes, Mü-Tsing."

"I thought you did not like the rose. So you ought not to like the good things it makes."

"But Mü-Tsing, tell me why did the rose god make the rose grow with so many thorns? Other flowers are not like that."

"Listen, dear child. If the rose tree were like other trees and still had its beautiful flowers, I think we should never have any for ourselves.

They would be too easily gathered. The rose god was very wise and put thorns all around his beautiful flower. When he made it, he gave it an odor so sweet that all the gods stopped working on the day it was finished. The thorns mean, 'Honor the rose, which grows forever. The cows cannot touch it, and the pigs never go near it, and careless children or wasteful people cannot destroy it.' Do you see, dear, why the rose must have thorns?"

The next morning Rose found in her room a beautiful new rose pillow made of the sweet-smelling petals. When she laid her head on this fragrant pillow, she said, "Mü-Tsing, I do not wish to change my name."

GLASSWARE: Cocktail glass

GARNISH: Dried rose petals

- 1½ oz. vodka or gin
- ¾ oz. Giffard Lichi-Li
- ¾ oz. fresh lemon juice
- ½ oz. lavender syrup
- ½ oz. Lillet Rouge
- ¾ oz. egg white
- 2 dashes rose water

1. Combine all of the ingredients in a cocktail shaker without ice and dry shake.

2. Add ice to shaker, shake again, and then strain into the cocktail glass.

3. Garnish with the dried rose petals.

LOST ORIENT

GENERAL LEE'S

The Oregon-brewed sake in this recipe is creamy with aromatic notes of vanilla, banana, and pineapple, imparting this drink with the quality of being lost in the best ways possible.

GLASSWARE: Chilled cocktail glass
GARNISH: Sesame oil, sesame seeds

- **1 oz. Espadín mezcal**
- **1 oz. Momokawa "Pearl" Nigori Saké**
- **1 oz. fresh lemon juice**
- **¾ oz. Black Sesame Syrup**
- **1 dash egg white**

1. Combine all of the ingredients in a cocktail shaker and dry shake.

2. Add ice, shake again, and strain into the chilled cocktail glass.

3. Garnish with the sesame oil and seeds.

BLACK SESAME SYRUP: Simmer ½ cup black sesame seeds in 2L water for 10 minutes. Strain, then add equal parts sugar to make a simple syrup.

LITTLE TOKYO

REDBIRD

Neal and Amy Knoll Fraser's Redbird serves "modern American" cuisine out of an old grand cathedral in historic downtown, creating a timeless atmosphere with a celebrated wine and bar menu curated by Tobin Shea. Shea, a proponent of classic cocktails, has won several awards for his creations, and the popular Little Tokyo is a celebratory drink initially made "to honor and celebrate our friends and neighbors" back during Redbird's opening.

GLASSWARE: Chilled rocks glass

- 1½ oz. nigori saké
- 1 oz. Cappelletti Bitters
- ¾ oz. sweet vermouth
- ¼ oz. yuzu juice

1. Combine all of the ingredients in a mixing glass with ice, stir until chilled, then strain into the chilled rocks glass over ice.

REDEYE

Between the coffee and the maple syrup, if you are looking for a morning cocktail, this Tobin Shea creation isn't a bad place to start.

GLASSWARE: Rocks glass

GARNISH: Orange twist

- **2 oz. bourbon**
- **½ oz. maple syrup**
- **½ oz. cold brew coffee**
- **4 drops Bitter End Memphis BBQ Bitters**

1. Combine all of the ingredients in a mixing glass with ice, stir until chilled, then strain into the rocks glass over a large ice cube.

2. Garnish with the orange twist.

GRAND MASTER RECORDS

Stevie Wonder, The Foo Fighters, David Bowie—the list of artists who spent time in this space before it was converted into a restaurant and bar, with a stunning rooftop perch looking onto the Hollywood Hills, is staggering. And that musical mojo lingers in the décor and the rock 'n' roll attitude behind both the food and drinks menus.

BRUSHFIRE FAIRYTALES

GRAND MASTER RECORDS

Beverage director Milosz Cieslak enjoys working with gin, which shows in this crisp, fruity drink.

GLASSWARE: Coupe
GARNISH: Torched rosemary sprig

- 1 oz. Sipsmith Gin
- ½ oz. St. George Spiced Pear Liqueur
- ¼ oz. vermouth blanc
- ½ oz. fresh lemon juice
- ¾ oz. pear puree
- 3 dashes celery bitters

1. Combine all of the ingredients in a cocktail shaker with ice, shake well, and strain into the coupe.

2. Garnish with the torched rosemary sprig.

NEGRONI CAFFE

GLASSWARE: Rocks glass
GARNISH: Orange peel

- 1 oz. The Botanist Gin
- ½ oz. espresso-infused Campari
- ½ oz. sweet vermouth
- ¾ oz. Mr. Black Cold Brew Coffee Liqueur
- 1 dash Aztec chocolate bitters

1. Combine all of the ingredients in a cocktail shaker with ice, shake well, and strain into the rocks glass.

2. Garnish with the orange peel.

MARTINI

MUSSO & FRANK

If these walls could talk, we'd be able to hear the ultimate unauthorized biography of Hollywood. But best to keep the secrets so we can enjoy the kind of place that is often imitated but never equaled. And this is a stone-cold classic cocktail from a place that has been pouring it for over 100 years. Heed this expert advice: do not shake; shaking adds ice crystals to the liquor, which ruins the texture of the drink.

GLASSWARE: Cocktail glass and small glass carafe
GARNISH: Pimiento-stuffed olives or lemon twist

- **4 oz. vodka or gin of your choice**

1. Pour the liquor into a mixing glass containing ice up to the rim.

2. Stir until the sides of the mixing glass are frosted.

3. Strain the drink into the cocktail glass, filling it to the rim, and finish with the preferred garnish.

4. Pour the rest of the martini into the glass carafe, which should be kept chilled on crushed ice.

GARRA DE TIGRE

GUELAGUETZA

Legendary food writer Jonathan Gold dubbed this temple of Oaxacan culture and cuisine "the best restaurant in the country." If that's not enough to get you there, how about some stellar cocktails? Bricia Lopez is a co-owner of Guelaguetza and her uncle, Abel Lopez, created the Garra de Tigre in Oaxaca.

GLASSWARE: Chile Sale–rimmed pint glass
GARNISH: 1 lime, halved

• **2 oz. mezcal**

• **2 tbsps. simple syrup**

1. Rub the rim of the cocktail glass with a lime half, dip the glass into the Chile Sale, and set aside.

2. Combine all of the ingredients with 1 cup ice in a blender and blend until smooth.

3. Pour the drink into the prepared glass and garnish with the other lime half.

CHILE SALE: Combine ¼ tsp. chile powder with 2 tbsps. coarse salt.

OAXACA SELTZER

A long with the deep flavors of mole, Oaxaca is known for mezcal, which makes this a perfect sipper to accompany. . .well, pretty much anything.

GLASSWARE: Rocks glass

- 1½ oz. mezcal
- 2 oz. fresh grapefruit juice
- ½ oz. fresh lime juice
- ½ oz. agave syrup
- Sparkling water, to top
- 4 drops Saline Solution (see page 181), to top
- 1 dash bitters, to top

1. Combine the mezcal, juices, and agave in the rocks glass, add a large ice cube, top with the sparkling water, saline, and bitters, and stir.

THE WESTSIDE

BOA STEAKHOUSE	THE ABBEY
BOSSA NOVA	THE ROGER ROOM
DELILAH	BARI
FORMOSA	ELLA'S
GRACIAS MADRE	HELEN'S WINES
HARRIET'S	PETTY CASH
KATANA	FANNY'S
BICYCLETTE	RÉPUBLIQUE
MANZKE	NOSTALGIA BAR AND LOUNGE
MONDRIAN SKY BAR	

Los Angeles is a city of abundance, from its demographic diversity to its varied landscapes. This part of the city butts up against the Santa Monica Mountains in Topanga State Park and the Pacific Ocean. There is something for everyone in this part of the city.

SMOKE SHOW

Tara Shadzi is an acclaimed bartender at celebrity hot spot BOA Steakhouse. Training with bar chefs like Tony Abou-Ganim, Dale DeGroff, and John Lamar inspired her to master the craft of the cocktail, and recent reviews have lauded her as one of the best mixologists in the city. This particular hit came to her during a visit to the bourbon distilleries of Louisville, Kentucky. At BOA, there is actual smoke involved with the presentation, but this recipe skips that step—yet another reason to make a trip to Los Angeles.

GLASSWARE: Rocks glass

GARNISH: Luxardo maraschino cherry

- 3 oz. Knob Creek Rye
- ⅓ oz. Grade A maple syrup
- ⅓ oz. water
- 2 dashes Scrappy's Orange Bitters
- 1 dash Angostura Bitters

1. Combine all of the ingredients in a cocktail shaker, shake well, and then funnel it into a small bottle; refrigerate the bottle.

2. Serve the chilled bottle alongside a rocks glass filled with a sphere ice cube, pour the cocktail into the glass, and garnish with the cherry.

RABO DE GALO

Bossa Nova, a Brazilian restaurant, is passionate about their food and drink. All ingredients are handpicked by the owners before reaching the bar menu, and the staff strives to deliver the best of Brazil in an West Hollywood setting. Bartender Robbie Reza's Rabo de Galo is a take on the traditional Brazilian cocktail that connects the sweet and fruity flavors of Don Papa Rum with the texture and nuttiness of cashews.

GLASSWARE: Rocks glass

GARNISH: Orange twist

- 1½ oz. Don Papa Rum
- ½ oz. sweet vermouth
- ¾ oz. Lo-Fi Vermouth
- ½ oz. cashew syrup
- 2 dashes Angostura Bitters

1. Combine all of the ingredients in a cocktail shaker with ice, shake well, and strain into the rocks glass over a large ice cube.

2. Garnish with the orange twist.

JOJO

DELILAH

Delilah prides itself on a contemporary take on the clubs of the roaring 1920s. The Jojo, named after a close friend and early supporter of Delilah's cofounders John Terzian and Brian Toll, is a stylish cocktail tailored to that unique atmosphere, pairing perfectly with the restaurant's supper club concept, interior aesthetics, and lounge vibes.

GLASSWARE: Champagne coupe

GARNISH: Amarena Fabbri, 1 strawberry

- 1½ oz. Sunny Vodka
- ½ oz. St. Germain
- 1 oz. Mixolojuice Lemon Juice
- ¾ oz. Mixolojuice Strawberry Syrup
- 1 dash Peychaud's Bitters
- Prosecco, to top

1. Combine all of the ingredients, except the prosecco, in a mixing glass with ice, stir, and then fine-strain into the coupe.

2. Top with the Prosecco, then garnish with the Amarena Fabbri and strawberry.

EL VENCIDO

FORMOSA

L ike so much of what is great about Los Angeles today, Formosa is a marvelous mash-up of histories. The likes of Frank Sinatra, Humphrey Bogart, and Ava Gardner would settle into the red leather booths in the original club, which opened in 1939 right across from Samuel Goldwyn Studio. The Hollywood lounge vibe remains, but now you can also eat what many consider to be the best Chinese food in West Hollywood, and drink cocktails inspired by Mexican flavors, like El Vencido.

GLASSWARE: Rocks glass

GARNISH: Orange slice

- **2 oz. Pueblo Viejo Blanco Tequila**
- **½ oz. Amaro di Angostura**
- **½ oz. pomegranate liqueur**
- **½ oz. Liquid Alchemist Prickly Pear Syrup**
- **½ oz. fresh lemon juice**

1. Combine all of the ingredients in a cocktail shaker with ice, shake well, and strain into the rocks glass over crushed ice.

2. Garnish with the orange slice.

OMUKASHI

FORMOSA

"Junmai" means "pure rice" and describes a sake made with only rice, koji, yeast, and water. This saké plays well with the gin, making for a very clean tasting cocktail.

GLASSWARE: Rocks glass

GARNISH: Orange peel

- 2 oz. Heaven's Sake Junmai 12 Saké
- ¾ oz. Bitter Truth Falernum
- 1 oz. Fords Gin
- 2 dashes orange bitters

1. Combine all of the ingredients in a mixing glass with ice, stir, and strain into the rocks glass over ice.

2. Garnish with the orange peel.

PURISTA MARGARITA

Gracias Madre is a Mexican restaurant with a twist: all of the menu items are plant-based. Fear not, however, the traditional flavors and preparations are front and center. Intrigued and can't get there for a meal? Be sure to check out *The Gracias Madre Cookbook*. But Maxwell Reis doesn't stray far from tradition for his version of a margarita, which serves two.

GLASSWARE: 2 Chile Salt–rimmed rocks glasses

GARNISH: Lime wheel or jalapeño slices

- **4 oz. blanco tequila or mezcal**
- **2 oz. fresh lime juice**
- **¾ oz. Agave Syrup**
- **4 dashes orange bitters**

1. Combine all of the ingredients in a cocktail shaker with ice, shake well, and strain into the prepared glasses over ice.

2. Garnish each drink with a lime wheel or jalapeño slice, depending on preference.

CHILE SALT: In a jar, combine ½ cup Himalayan salt and 2 tsps. chipotle powder, mix well, and store, covered, for up to 1 month.

AGAVE SYRUP: In a bowl, combine ⅔ cup agave nectar and ⅓ cup boiling water and mix well. Let cool and transfer to a squeeze bottle.

SPICY SIENA

HARRIET'S

On Harriet's West Hollywood rooftop, the Spicy Siena is the perfect cocktail to enjoy the views and sunset happy hours. It's named after the wife of Brian Toll, a Harriet's cofounder who helped come up with the drink when the group opened their first restaurant, The Nice Guy. Ever since, it's been a hit at the bar of all their venues.

GLASSWARE: Tajín-rimmed rocks glass

GARNISH: 2 Fresno chile rings, deseeded

- 2 oz. 818 Tequila Blanco
- ½ oz. Cointreau
- 1 oz. Mixolojuice Lime Juice
- ½ oz. agave syrup (2:1)
- 4 Fresno chiles, cut into rings and deseeded

1. Combine all of the ingredients in a cocktail shaker and muddle the chiles, then shake vigorously and strain into the rocks glass over ice.

2. Garnish with 2 chile slices.

SHINJUKU GARDENS

KATANA

Katana general manager Jasmine Garcia has been making cocktails for over ten years, and, she says, they will always be her top passion. This one takes its name from Shinjuku, one of the twenty-three city wards of Tokyo, known for the large entertainment, business, and shopping area around its train station. The area's spacious parks and meandering paths make for tranquil scenery and a relaxing escape from the busy urbanity around it, and this cocktail taps into that feeling—it's an ultimate refresher with herbaceous notes and a subtle sweet-and-light flavor.

GLASSWARE: Sugar-rimmed collins glass
GARNISH: Matcha, pumpkin- and mint-leaf bouquet lime wheel, and an edible flower

- 2 cucumber slices
- 2 oz. Beluga Vodka
- ½ oz. Midori
- ½ oz. maraschino cherry liqueur
- ¾ oz. fresh lemon juice
- ½ oz. simple syrup
- Fever-Tree Sparkling Lime & Yuzu Tonic Water, to top

1. Combine all of the ingredients, except the tonic water, in a cocktail shaker, muddle the cucumbers, shake well, and strain into the Collins glass over ice.

2. Top with the tonic water and then garnish with the matcha, leaves, lime wheel, and flower.

BICYCLETTE

Bicyclette Bistro is the newest Parisian-inspired restaurant from chefs Walter and Margarita Manzke. Fusing Paris's iconic bistro culture with California's fresh ingredients, their cocktails will transplant you to Paris without leaving Los Angeles.

GLASSWARE: Rocks glass

GARNISH: Thinly sliced cucumbers and lime zest

- **3 Persian cucumber slices**
- **1 oz. fresh lime juice**
- **¾ oz. Cucumber-Infused Pernod Absinthe (see page 126)**
- **¾ oz. Château de Ravignan Floc de Gascogne**
- **¾ oz. Orgeat (see page 126)**
- **2 dashes celery (see page 126) bitters**
- **2 dashes Saline Solution (see page 181)**

1. Muddle the cucumbers with the lime juice in a cocktail shaker.

2. Add all of the other ingredients to the shaker with 1 oz. pebble ice, shake well, and fine-strain into the rocks glass over pebble ice.

3. Garnish with the thinly sliced cucumbers and lime zest.

CUCUMBER-INFUSED PERNOD ABSINTHE: In a container with a lid, combine 300g thinly sliced Persian cucumbers with 1 (750ml) bottle Pernod Absinthe. Let steep for 24 hours, then fine-strain and store.

ORGEAT: Combine 800ml toasted almond milk, 820g evaporated cane sugar, 20g Amaretto Lazzaroni, 20g cognac, and 20 drops orange flower water in a blender and process on medium speed for 2 minutes, or until the sugar has dissolved. Bottle the mixture and refrigerate for up to 2 weeks.

SHAWN LICKLITER

Shawn Lickliter is one of the foremost bartenders in Los Angeles, and, since 2014, he has been the beverage director for chefs Walter and Magarita Manzke's properties, which include Republique, Manzke, Bicyclette Bistro, Petty Cash Taqueria, and Sari Sari Store. A self-taught bartender from eastern Tennessee, Lickliter originally came to Los Angeles as a touring musician. Like many musicians, he would often take on bartending gigs between tours, and over many shaken cocktails, late nights, and more-than-colorful patrons, began to realize that this might be his calling.

Lickliter continued to hone his craft and eventually landed at the esteemed Beverly Hills restaurant Bouchon, working alongside some of the city's culinary greats. He then found employment with the highly respected Manzkes, who have been instrumental in giving Lickliter multiple venues to demonstrate his curiosity, ingenuity, and disci-

pline. Lickliter has made a name for himself and these establishments, and, along with other talent in the city, has helped to define the conversation around cocktails and their vital role in Los Angeles' nightlife.

Lickliter personally oversees the bar programs and staff at all five properties with exacting detail, and you can often find him behind the bar at these restaurants bringing his renowned cocktails to life. He has been a pioneer in advocating for independent producers, and partners with brands that not only provide the highest quality output, but also produce their spirits in the most sustainable ways possible.

Prior to the opening of Bicyclette Bistro, Lickliter and Walter Manzke started to think creatively about how to further elevate a bar program, which led to their interest in procuring vintage spirits. Through estate sales, auctions, and brokers, Lickliter has acquired often rare and near-impossible-to-find spirits, with a specific focus on European whiskey, American whiskey, and brandy dating as far back as the 1930s. Today, guests can try these exclusive spirits for themselves at Manzke.

Lickliter continues to push boundaries and is considered one of Los Angeles' most respected, talented, and innovative wine and spirits professionals.

HAZELNUT COCKTAIL

MANZKE

Above their bistro Bicyclette, chefs Walter and Margarita Manzke run a separate tasting menu—the Manzke Restaurant. Here, dishes are made from all the many ingredients found on Los Angeles' cultural crossroads, drawing inspiration from the cuisines of Latin America, Asia, and Europe alike, and the Hazelnut Cocktail is a staple on its bar menu.

GLASSWARE: Rocks glass

- 1 oz. Hazelnut-Infused Macallan 12 Year Sherry Oak Whisky (see page 130)
- 1 oz. Hazelnut-Infused Lustau Solera Gran Reserva Brandy (see page 130)
- ½ oz. Harmless Harvest Coconut Water
- ¼ oz. coconut liqueur
- ½ tsp. rich demerara syrup (2:1 sugar to water)
- 2 dashes aromatic bitters

1. Combine all of the ingredients in a mixing glass with ice, stir to chill, and then strain into the rocks glass over a large ice cube.

HAZELNUT-INFUSED MACALLAN 12 YEAR SHERRY OAK WHISKY: Spread 200g hazelnut paste across the bottom of a large, deep pan. Pour 1 (750ml) bottle Macallan 12 Year Sherry Oak Whisky over the top and let it infuse for 24 hours at room temperature. Strain the infused spirit into a new container and freeze overnight. When the hazelnut fat has solidified, strain the infusion through a cheesecloth or coffee filter, bottle, and refrigerate.

HAZELNUT-INFUSED LUSTAU SOLERA GRAN RESERVA BRANDY: Spread 200g hazelnut paste across the bottom of a large, deep pan. Pour 1 (750ml) bottle Lustau Solera Gran Reserva Brandy over the top and let it infuse for 24 hours at room temperature. Strain the infused spirit into a new container and freeze overnight. When the hazelnut fat has solidified, strain the infusion through a cheesecloth or coffee filter, bottle, and refrigerate.

MONDRIAN MARGARITA

MONDRIAN SKY BAR

Whether you're lounging poolside by day or vibing to the beats late into the night, both the views and the cocktails at this rooftop bar are exceptional.

GLASSWARE: Tumbler with salted rim

GARNISH: Lime wheel

- 1 oz. Avion Silver Tequila
- ½ oz. Giffard Triple Sec
- ¾ oz. fresh lime juice
- ¼ oz. organic agave
- ½ oz. orange juice

1. Add all of the ingredients to a cocktail shaker with ice, shake well, and strain into the prepared glass.

2. Garnish with the lime wheel.

REDHEADED MULE

This fruity riff on a classic Moscow Mule is incredibly easy to sip after a final dip in the pool before the sun sets.

GLASSWARE: Rocks glass
GARNISH: Lime wheel, raspberries

- **6 raspberries**
- **2 oz. Ketel One Vodka**
- **½ oz. simple syrup**
- **½ oz. fresh lemon juice**
- **Ginger beer, to top**

1. Muddle the raspberries in a cocktail shaker, and then add the remainder of the ingredients, except the ginger beer, with ice, shake well, and pour into the rocks glass.

2. Top with the ginger beer and garnish with the lime wheel and raspberries.

RASPBERRY MOJITO

D avid Cooley's West Hollywood gay bar prides itself on the meticulous craftsmanship of its in-house cocktail syrups and juice mixes. The Abbey's many accolades include MTV's "Best Gay Bar in the World," Zagat's "Most Popular Nightlife Destination in Los Angeles," and Foursquare's "Most Popular Bar in California." Among the choices on its celebrated bar menu, the martinis and mojitos move fastest, and the Raspberry Mojito is no exception.

GLASSWARE: Collins glass

GARNISH: Mint leaves, lime wedge, and sugarcane

- 10 mint leaves
- 5 raspberries
- 4 lime wedges
- 2 oz. Bacardí Raspberry
- ½ oz. simple syrup
- Soda water, to top

1. Muddle the mint leaves, raspberries, and freshly squeezed lime wedges in a cocktail shaker.

2. Add the rum and simple syrup to the shaker along with ice, top with the soda water, and shake well.

3. Pour the drink into the Collins glass and garnish with the mint leaves, lime wedge, and sugarcane.

CHAI WHISKEY SOUR

This Danny Vasquez creation has a wonderful texture thanks to the egg whites, and the freshly grated cinnamon and star anise play well with the chai simple syrup.

GLASSWARE: Coupe

GARNISH: Grated cinnamon, star anise

- **2 oz. Buffalo Trace Bourbon**
- **¾ oz. chai simple syrup**
- **1 oz. fresh lemon juice**
- **Generous pour of egg whites**

1. Combine all of the ingredients in a cocktail shaker with ice, shake well, and strain into the coupe.

2. Garnish with the grated cinnamon and star anise

BARI MARTINI

BARI

Y ou don't need an olive in your Martini when your gin has been flavored with olive oil.

◇❋◇

GLASSWARE: Nick and Nora glass
GARNISH: 1 or 2 olive leaves

- **3 oz. Olive Oil Washed Gin**
- **1 lemon peel**

1. Stir the gin over ice in a mixing glass and strain into the Nick and Nora glass.

2. Express the lemon peel, rub it on the glass rim, and discard.

3. Garnish with the olive leaves.

OLIVE OIL WASHED GIN: Combine 1 liter premium gin and 4 oz. Centonze Extra Virgin Olive Oil (or another premium extra virgin olive oil) in a container with a lid and freeze overnight. Discard the frozen oil, stir in 4 oz. dry vermouth, and store in a bottle.

AMERICANO RABARBARO

BARI

Chinotto Polara is a slightly sour Italian soda made from bitter orange extract and other flavors.

GLASSWARE: Rocks glass

GARNISH: Half wheel of blood orange

- 1 oz. Campari
- 1 oz. sweet vermouth
- Chinotto Polara, to top
- Soda water, to top

1. Add ice to the rocks glass and then add the Campari and vermouth.

2. Top off with a 50/50 blend of the Chinotto Polara and soda water and garnish with the half wheel of blood orange.

CACTUS PRICK

Pulling from the bistro culture of Europe and New York, Ella's relaxed and jazzy atmosphere engenders an elevated sense of comfort. It's a place you feel you've been to before, yet there is nothing else like it in Los Angeles. Zach Patterson and Dorian de Tappan's bar menu captures the taste of local culture with an Ella's twist. The Cactus Prick has followed de Tappan throughout the bartending world, evolving with his skills, but its basic structure and intention have remained consistent: activate all five tastes, twice. The echo is the goal.

GLASSWARE: Tajín-rimmed rocks glass
GARNISH: Dehydrated lime wheel, red chile thread

- 2 oz. Piña-infused Mezcal 400 Conejos
- ¾ oz. English cucumber juice
- ½ oz. ginger syrup (1:1 ginger juice and evaporated cane sugar)
- ¾ oz. fresh lime juice
- ¾ oz. avocado agave puree
- 1 dash Angostura Bitters
- 1 spritz orange extract, to top
- 1 spritz Ardbeg Scotch, to top

1. Combine all of the ingredients, except the orange extract and Scotch, in a cocktail shaker with ice, give it a medium shake, and strain into the prepared rocks glass over ice.

2. Garnish with the dehydrated lime wheel and a nest of red chile threads, then spray with the orange extract and Ardbeg Scotch.

MELON ROSE SANGRIA

HELEN'S WINES

In 2016, *Food & Wine* named Helen Johannesen Best New Sommelier, so it stands to reason that her eponymous wine shop at the back of Jon & Vinny's (where she serves as beverage director) is big on wonderful grapey surprises, even if the space is small. Needless to say, since this is Los Angeles, this recipe will be best when the summer melons are at their peak.

GLASSWARE: Pitcher and highball glasses

- **10 tbsps. honeydew**
- **10 tbsps. watermelon**
- **4 sliced strawberries**
- **½ lemon**

- **1 (750ml) bottle inexpensive dry rosé**
- **6 oz. 7UP or white grapefruit juice**

1. Add the fruit to the pitcher and squeeze in the lemon.

2. Add the wine and 7UP or juice, fill with ice, and stir.

ORANGE WINE SPRITZ

I f you can't visit Helen's in person to get a recommendation for the best wine to use in this recipe, ask your favorite local wine merchant.

GLASSWARE: Goblet

GARNISH: Thin lemon slices, 2 fresh tarragon leaves

- ½ lemon
- 2 oz. tropical orange, floral wine
- 2 oz. skin contact/unfiltered Prosecco
- 1 oz. Aperol
- 2 fresh tarragon leaves

1. Squeeze the lemon into the goblet, then add the remainder of the ingredients and ice and stir.

2. Garnish with the lemon slices along the inside of the glass.

3. Slap the tarragon leaves between your hands to release the aromatics, tear the leaves in half, and add them to the top of the drink.

PICA FRESA

Named in honor of Johnny Cash and Tom Petty (and the cover band that plays their hits), Petty Cash is a taqueria created by Walter Manzke. He credits a youth spent taking trips to Tijuana and its tacos, tequila, and music for the idea and the cocktail menu.

GLASSWARE: Coupe
GARNISH: Ground chipotle

- 1½ oz. El Tesoro Blanco Tequila
- ½ oz. Cucumber Syrup
- ½ oz. Pickled Strawberry and Fresno Chile Brine
- ½ oz. fresh lemon juice

1. Combine all of the ingredients in a cocktail shaker with ice, shake well, and strain into the coupe.

2. Garnish with a dusting of the ground chipotle, to taste.

CUCUMBER SYRUP: Add 250g cucumber juice and 250g sugar to a blender and emulsify until the sugar has dissolved. Refrigerate to store.

PICKLED STRAWBERRY AND FRESNO CHILE BRINE: Combine 250g white balsamic vinegar, 250g water, 5g salt, and 50g sugar in a saucepan and bring to a boil. Pour the solution over 10 hulled and quartered strawberries and 2 seeded and sliced Fresno chiles in a heatproof container. Allow to cool to room temperature, then refrigerate to store.

THE WORLD'S BEST MARTINI

FANNY'S

In the heart of the Academy Museum of Motion Pictures is Fanny's, a restaurant and café named after Fanny Brice, the famous American actress and comedienne immortalized by Barbra Streisand's Oscar-winning portrayal in 1968's *Funny Girl*. Behind its bar is mixologist Julian Cox, one of *Food & Wine*'s top ten bartenders of the 2010s and the mind behind The World's Best Martini. "The Kastra Elion Vodka is super specific," he says, "because it's made from olives." The Ki No Bi gin "has a rice-based spirit, and the two balance each other out beautifully, like an old married couple."

GLASSWARE: Frozen cocktail glass seasoned with a lemon twist
GARNISH: Castelvetrano olives, Salted Yuzu Essence

- 1½ oz. Kastra Elion Vodka
- 1½ oz. Kio No Bi Kyoto Dry Gin
- ¾ oz. Dolin Dry Vermouth
- 1 dash Regan's Orange Bitters
- 1 dash Japanese yuzu bitters
- 1 dash Fanny's Saline Tincture

1. Combine all of the ingredients in a mixing glass with ice, stir, and strain into the prepared cocktail glass.

2. Garnish with the Castelvetrano olives and a spritz of Salted Yuzu Essence.

Salted Yuzu Essence: In a large container, combine 1 (750ml) bottle Boyd & Blair Proof 151, 6.8g yuzu juice, and 30g Hawaiian black salt and use an immersion blender until the salt dissolves.

Fanny's Saline Tincture: Mix 20g kosher salt into 100g water and stir thoroughly.

STRAWBERRY COCKTAIL

RÉPUBLIQUE

Another of Walter and Margarita Manzke's creations, République is a French-inspired restaurant on the Miracle Mile in the heart of Los Angeles.

GLASSWARE: Rocks glass

GARNISH: Cilantro blossoms

- 2 Harry's Berries strawberries
- 1 oz. fresh lemon juice
- 1½ oz. Lime Leaf Gin
- ½ oz. Lo-Fi Amaro
- ½ oz. Strawberry Cordial
- 2 dashes Scrappy's Grapefruit Bitters

1. Add the strawberries and lemon juice to a cocktail shaker and muddle them.

2. Add the remainder of the ingredients to the cocktail shaker, with ice, shake well, and fine-strain into the rocks glass over a large ice cube.

3. Garnish with the cilantro blossoms.

LIME LEAF GIN: Combine 25g makrut lime leaves with 1000ml Resetbauer Blue Gin in an iSi canister. Charge it twice using N₂O chargers, shaking between each charge. Allow to infuse for 25 minutes and then vent quickly by squeezing the nozzle to release all the gas. Unscrew the top of the canister and let the liquid rest until the bubbles have subsided. Fine-strain and refrigerate.

STRAWBERRY CORDIAL: Combine 250g hulled and quartered Harry's Berries Strawberries, 250g evaporated cane sugar, 1g salt, and 2½g citric acid in a sous vide bag and cryovac to compress. Fill a large basin with water and attach an immersion circulator set to 180°F. Sous vide the mixture for 2 hours, then transfer to a blender with 250g simple syrup. Blend until smooth and then fine-strain through a chinois. Refrigerate and use within 1 week.

VIOLETS ARE BLUE

NOSTALGIA BAR AND LOUNGE

Chris Sayegh, aka The Herbal Chef, opened Nostalgia Bar and Lounge with a clear mission in mind: to evoke the sensibilities of childhood. This is done, in part, with a food and drinks menu that pairs food memories like Capri Sun and Orange Julius with CBD- and terpene-infused cocktails. For some of those recipes, check out The Herbal Chef's cookbook, *Sugar High*. In the meantime, try this Bianca Sterling creation, which has a wonderful adult-juice-box quality to it.

GLASSWARE: Oversized coupe
GARNISH: Expressed lemon oil, dehydrated lemon wheel,
edible violet flower

- 1¾ oz. Nelson's Green Brier Tennessee Whiskey
- ½ oz. Red Wine Reduction
- ½ oz. Chambord Black Raspberry Liqueur
- ½ oz. Giffard Crème de Violette
- ⅓ oz. Giffard Wild Elderflower Liqueur
- ½ oz. Blueberry Purée
- ¾ oz. fresh lemon juice
- 1 oz. egg white
- 2 drops Saline Solution (see page 181)

1. Combine all of the ingredients in a cocktail shaker and dry shake for 1 minute.

2. Add ice, shake well, and double strain into the coupe.

3. Garnish with the expressed lemon oil (peel discarded), dehydrated lemon wheel, and edible violet flower.

RED WINE REDUCTION: Simmer red wine of choice and reduce to half its volume, then combine 1 part wine reduction with 1 part organic cane sugar and mix until sugar dissolves.

BLUEBERRY PURÉE: Purée blueberries, then dilute 1 part blueberry purée with 1 part water.

EXCHANGE STUDENT

L illet Blanc is French, but the other spirits in this cocktail are Italian, so perhaps Chris Serrano should have called this one The Italian Exchange Student?

GLASSWARE: Hawaiian sea salt–rimmed rocks glass

- 1 oz. Cynar 70 Amaro
- 1 oz. Punt e Mes Vermouth
- ¾ oz. Cucumber-Infused Campari
- ½ oz. Lillet Blanc
- ¼ oz. maraschino cherry liqueur

1. Combine all of the ingredients in a mixing glass with ice and stir to combine.

2. Strain into the prepared rocks glass over a large ice cube.

CUCUMBER-INFUSED CAMPARI: Peel and chop 1 large organic cucumber. In an airtight container, combine the chopped cucumber with 1L Campari and infuse for 1 week. Strain and store.

THE EASTSIDE

CAPRI CLUB

CHIFA

GENEVER

THUNDERBOLT

THE AIRLINER

BIG BAR

ALL DAY BABY

The precise parameters of this part of Los Angeles are a bit porous. But one thing is for certain: there is no shortage of excellent bars.

MEZCALETTI SOUR

CAPRI CLUB

The Capri Club—"Eagle Rock's Aperitivo Bar"—originally opened as The Capri in 1963 and was run by two different families until 2019, when new owner Robert Fleming renovated and renamed the place while staying true to its storied history. All of beverage director Nic Vascocu's cocktails, like this one, embrace a very Italian way of drinking.

GLASSWARE: Rocks glass

GARNISH: Lemon peel, 1 cherry

- **1½ oz. Meletti Amaro**
- **1 oz. mezcal**
- **½ oz. Liquid Alchemist Orgeat**
- **¼ oz. House Red Bitter Blend**
- **1 oz. fresh lemon juice**
- **3 drops Saline Solution (see page 181)**

1. Combine all of the ingredients in a cocktail shaker with ice, shake well, and strain into the rocks glass over ice.

2. Garnish with the lemon peel and cherry.

Capri
CLUB

4604 EAGLE ROCK BLVD.
LOS ANGELES, CALIF.
90041

COPPOLA

CAPRI CLUB

Like the drink's famed namesake, the rye makes this cocktail a truly Italian-American invention.

GLASSWARE: Chalice

GARNISH: Lemon twist

- 1½ oz. rye whiskey
- ½ oz. Averna Amaro
- ½ oz. Brucato Chaparral Amaro
- 2 dashes orange bitters
- 2 dashes Peychaud's Bitters
- 2 drops Saline Solution (see page 181)

1. Combine all of the ingredients in a mixing glass with ice, stir well, and strain into the chalice.

2. Garnish with the lemon twist.

PALOMA SHIMMER

This Cantonese-Peruvian restaurant, originally opened by Wendy Leon in Lima in 1975, serves up drinks that perfectly complement the incredible fusion food menu.

GLASSWARE: Tumbler

GARNISH: Edible glitter

- 1½ oz. tequila
- 2½ oz. grapefruit juice
- 1 oz. simple syrup
- ½ oz. fresh lemon or lime juice
- Soda water, to top

1. Add all of the ingredients, except the soda water, to the tumbler with ice and stir well.

2. Top with the soda water and garnish with the edible glitter.

THE MANDARIN

CHIFA

f you like drinks on the bubbly side of things, this one's for you.

GLASSWARE: Rocks glass

- 1½ oz. sparkling wine
- ¾ oz. Aperol
- ½ oz. simple syrup
- ½ oz. fresh lime juice
- Soda water, to top

1. Add the sparkling wine, Aperol, simple syrup, and lime juice to the rocks glass with ice, stir well, and top with the soda water.

GENEVER

Genever is a boutique cocktail bar founded and owned by three Filipino-American women: Patricia Perez, Roselma Samala, and Christine Sumiller. Their aim in creating Genever was to offer a welcoming environment where women could feel comfortable by themselves or with friends, to promote the Filipino cultural heritage of the owners, and to challenge the notions of what women typically drink. Helping Genever with all this is beverage director Kelso Norris, a musician, cocktail expert, and student of the legendary bartender Meaghan Dorman.

TELEPHONE CALL FROM ISTANBUL

GENEVER

Co-owner Roselma Samala's pick is the Telephone Call from Istanbul, an early Genever creation, which she appreciates for its "sweet, bitter, and sour flavors," which are "deeply connected with memories of joy and adventure, and the skill of its creator, Kelso Norris."

GLASSWARE: Nick and Nora glass

GARNISH: Rose water spritz, rosebud

- 1½ oz. Plymouth Gin
- 1 oz. Martini & Rossi Ambrato Vermouth
- ½ oz. pomegranate molasses
- ¼ oz. Small Hands Foods Almond Orgeat

1. Combine all of the ingredients in a cocktail shaker with ice, shake gently until chilled, and then strain into the Nick and Nora glass.

2. Spritz with the rose water and garnish with the rosebud.

NEW BIMINI PLACE

GENEVER

C o-owner Patricia Perez calls this one a "bright, clean, joyful, and unassuming cocktail that is a sexy, strong surprise." Domaine Brazilier is a dry sparkling wine.

GLASSWARE: Chilled Collins glass

GARNISH: Pomegranate arils

- 1 oz. Bimini Gin
- 1 oz. pomegranate-guava cordial
- ¾ oz. citrus blend (50/50 lemon/lime juice)
- 2 oz. Domaine Brazilier

1. Combine all of the ingredients, except the sparkling wine, in a cocktail shaker with ice, shake well, and strain into the chilled Collins glass over ice.

2. Top with the sparkling wine and garnish with the pomegranate arils.

SUMMER BABE

GENEVER

Christine "Tinette" Sumiller champions the Summer Babe, a Genever take on the white negroni; despite the name, it was originally featured during winter, which she says "can still feel like summer in Los Angeles." Kelso Norris, its creator, refers to the drink as an "extra wintery boost with frankincense and myrrh."

GLASSWARE: Rocks glass

GARNISH: Lemon twist

- 1 oz. Edinburgh Christmas Gin
- 1 oz. Lillet Blanc
- 1 oz. Amaro Angeleno
- 1 dash ginger bitters
- 1 dash saffron bitters

1. Combine all of the ingredients in the rocks glass with ice, stir until chilled, and garnish with the lemon twist.

P-TOWN BOXING CLUB

THUNDERBOLT

Thunderbolt is located in the Historic Filipinotown neighborhood of Los Angeles. Two of its founding partners, Johneric Concordia and Christine Araquel-Concordia, are also the owners of the legendary Filipino-American barbecue restaurant, The Park's Finest, and the founders of the P-Town Boxing Club. This eponymous cocktail is a collaboration between the Concordias and Thunderbolt owner/operator Michael Capoferri: it's a classic Filipino flavor pairing—coconut and pandan leaf —delivered in the format of the most familiar and approachable cocktail, the old-fashioned.

GLASSWARE: Double rocks glass
GARNISH: Oil from a lemon peel

- 2 oz. Coconut-Washed Bonded Rye Whiskey
- ½ oz. Pandan Syrup
- 2 dashes Angostura Bitters
- 3 drops Saline Solution (optional)

1. Combine all of the ingredients in the double rocks glass, add a large, clear ice cube, and stir for 15 to 20 seconds.

2. Garnish with a spritz of oil from the lemon peel.

COCONUT-WASHED BONDED RYE WHISKEY: In a vacuum bag, combine 200g unrefined virgin coconut oil and 750ml bonded rye whiskey, then seal. Cook sous vide in a water bath at 125°F for 1 hour, agitating every 20 minutes. Remove the bag from the water bath and transfer it to an ice bath to cool, then freeze until all of the coconut oil has solidified. Cut a small corner off the vacuum bag and strain the whiskey through a fine strainer.

PANDAN SYRUP: In a vacuum bag, combine 200g water, 200g granulated sugar, and 150g rough-chopped pandan leaf. Seal the bag, cook sous vide at 140°F for 1 hour, agitating every 20 minutes, then transfer to an ice bath. Once cooled, cut a small corner off the vacuum bag and strain the syrup.

SALINE SOLUTION: In a small container, combine 200g water and 50g salt. Stir until fully dissolved.

THE AIRLINER

The exact date The Airliner originally opened is a debate depending on who you ask, with dates ranging from 1923 to 1924. One thing not up for debate is that The Airliner, with its rich history, is ready to add to its legacy with a new chapter. The reimagined concept is the brainchild of partners Monica Blair and Sean Kelly, who brought in bar director Raul Pool for the new menu. Pool is a Los Angeles native with over a decade of bar experience in venues across the country. Now he's home, and he invites anyone to pull up a seat and join him at the bar. When asked about his work, Pool says, "Hospitality is a selfless industry. We are not in it for ourselves, but for the elevated experience we provide our guests day in, day out. I am here to coach my staff to a win every day, and this is a never-ending season."

OFF BROADWAY

THE AIRLINER

"With agave spirits being a focal point of my career," bar director Raul Pool explains, "the Off Broadway showcases two things: the star of the show—our menu—that is adjacent to the street our bar resides on, Broadway, and my favorite song by a band from my high school years, "Off Broadway" by Every Time I Die. It is my take on a slightly spicy passion fruit margarita with the Amaro to give it a bit of backbone. The tinctures I create are my spice rack and my way of adding flavors without overwhelming a cocktail. In this cocktail the spice is more of a hint than overwhelming."

GLASSWARE: Lime salt–rimmed rocks glass
GARNISH: Lime wheel

- 1½ oz. tequila
- ¼ oz. Lo-Fi Gentian Amaro
- ½ oz. Chinola Passion Fruit Liqueur
- ½ oz. fresh lime juice
- ¼ oz. agave syrup
- 2 dashes Chile de Arbol Tincture
- Orange twist

1. Combine all of the ingredients in a cocktail shaker with ice, shake well, and strain into the prepared rocks glass over ice.

2. Garnish with the lime wheel.

SUEDE

"This cocktail was inspired by my upbringing in Echo Park," bar director Pool says. "I wanted it to taste like an agua fresca. My upbringing made me so familiar with watermelon and honeydew in my bags full of fruit, lime, and Tajín from the fruit vendors circulating in the park, so I wanted to showcase cantaloupe in this cocktail and make it absolutely crushable. One of my favorite artists, Anderson Paak, inspired the name. When tasting it with my staff, the first thing we kept saying was, 'This cocktail is smoooth,' and one of the first lines in his song "Suede" evokes the same sentiment."

GLASSWARE: Double rocks glass
GARNISH: Grated lime zest

- 1¼ oz. gin
- ½ oz. Chareau Aloe Liqueur
- 1 oz. cantaloupe
- ¾ oz. fresh lemon juice
- ½ oz. simple syrup
- 3–4 dashes rhubarb bitters

1. Combine all of the ingredients in a cocktail shaker, dry shake, and then strain into the double rocks glass.

2. Add enough crushed ice so it forms a mound, then zest a lime over the top.

D.B. COOPER

THE AIRLINER

66 "T his cocktail," says bar director Raul Pool, "was created on a bespoke challenge from a guest using Oregon as a base. Being a history buff and a student of the spirit world, I used a single malt whiskey, Westward Whiskey, and made an Arnold Palmer/whiskey sour riff, using a homemade strawberry tea. In 1971, D.B. Cooper hijacked an airplane for ransom and jumped out over the state of Oregon, never to be seen again. This story ties into our bar's title, The Airliner, so I thought it was a fun trivia fact to use an Oregon-based spirit and name it after an enigmatic persona."

GLASSWARE: Collins glass

GARNISH: Lemon moon

- 1½ oz. Westward Whiskey
- 1 oz. fresh lemon juice
- ¾ oz. simple syrup
- 2 dashes Angostura Bitters
- ¾ oz. strawberry tea

1. Combine all of the ingredients, except the strawberry tea, in a cocktail shaker with ice, shake well, and strain into the Collins glass.

2. Add crushed ice to fill, then float the strawberry tea and garnish with the lemon moon.

PINKY SWEAR

L ounging on the patio or enjoying the ambiance of one of the oldest structures in Los Feliz, since opening in 2010, Big Bar has been crafting top-notch seasonal cocktails that take full advantage of the amazing variety of local produce available year-round, like the grapes used for this "olive" garnish.

GLASSWARE: Coupe

**GARNISH: Expressed oil from orange twist,
"Olive" on a pick (see page 190)**

- 1 oz. Singani 63
- 1 oz. Redemption Rye
- ¾ oz. Carpano Bianco Vermouth
- ¼ oz. maraschino cherry liqueur
- ¼ oz. martini bitters

1. Combine all of the ingredients in a cocktail shaker with ice, shake well, and strain into the coupe.

2. Express the orange twist over the drink, discard the twist, and add the "Olive" on a pick.

"OLIVES": Using a metal straw, core 20 plump green grapes to allow the pickling solution to saturate them. In a suitable container, combine 1 cup champagne vinegar, 1 cup baker's sugar, 1 cup water, 3 tbsps. salt, and 2 tbsps. black peppercorn. Mix well, add the grapes, and let them sit for at least a day before using.

PAINKILLER

ALL DAY BABY

J orge Figueroa, an Angeleno native of Guatemalan heritage, is the bar director of All Day Baby, a restaurant, bakery, and cocktail bar with the soul of a diner. He opened the restaurant in November 2019 and previously worked at its sister restaurant, Here's Looking At You. He explains how this drink was "born during the pandemic, when to-go drinks were popularized, so we put the drink into juice bottles, which made it very appealing to our guests. It's continued to be a favorite cocktail on the menu. The original Painkiller is a little too sweet for my taste, so I think the Chinola Passion Fruit Liqueur and strawberry float balance out the flavors and provide a fun twist." For the coconut cream, Coco Lopez works well, but Figueroa blends together equal parts Coco Lopez, sweet condensed coconut milk, and coconut water.

GLASSWARE: Hurricane glass

GARNISH: Parasol

- 1½ oz. SelvaRey White Rum
- ½ oz. Chinola Passion Fruit Liqueur
- 1½ oz. pineapple juice
- 1 oz. orange juice
- 1 oz. coconut cream
- ½ oz. fresh lime juice
- 1½ oz. strawberry puree

1. Combine all of the ingredients, except the strawberry puree, in a cocktail shaker with crushed ice, shake for 10 seconds, and pour into the hurricane glass.

2. Fill with more crushed ice, add a float of strawberry puree to the top of the drink, and watch as it beautifully trickles down the cocktail. Garnish with the cocktail parasol.

THE SOUTHSIDE

THE GATHERING SPOT

ALTA

CANOPY CLUB

CHAMP CITY BAR AND LOUNGE

ncluding areas like West Adams and Inglewood, home of SoFi Stadium, this part of the city beats with another vibrant pulse of Los Angeles culture, and cocktails.

HATTIE'S MELANGE

THE GATHERING SPOT

Rohana "Robi 1 Kanobi" Khalfani, a Brooklyn, New York, native who now happily calls California home, is a founding bartender at the Gathering Spot's LA location. A fan of sci-fi and artistic expression, she has been bartending for a decade with a focus on the elevation and celebration of Black spaces and cities through her hospitality. This drink came from a group effort with her team, playing around with flavors they all enjoyed. "The community," she says, "is what inspires creativity—especially for me."

GLASSWARE: Tajín-rimmed cocktail glass
GARNISH: Cucumber slice

- 2¼-inch cucumber slices
- 1¼-inch jalapeño slice (with seeds)
- ¾ oz. simple syrup
- 2 oz. San Bartolo Espadín Mezcal
- 1½ oz. fresh lime juice
- ¼ oz. pineapple juice
- 2 bar spoons dried rose petals

1. Muddle the cucumber, jalapeño, and simple syrup in a cocktail shaker.

2. Add the remainder of the ingredients, along with ice, shake well, and double strain into the prepared cocktail glass.

RASHAD JOY

Rashad Joy is a mixologist from Washington, DC, who started his craft there in the historically Black U Street neighborhood. But he mastered it in Los Angeles. He now slings his own creations as the beverage director of Alta, a critically acclaimed, Black-owned soul food restaurant in the heart of West Adams.

THE ANGELENO

ALTA

This is Rashad Joy's version of a Los Angeles Manhattan: sophisticated, rich, sweet, and sexy, but something that will still punch you in the face.

GLASSWARE: Coupe

GARNISH: Expressed orange peel, Luxardo maraschino cherry

- 2 oz. Four Roses Bourbon
- 1 oz. Amaro Montenegro

- 3 dashes Dashfire Mole Cacao & Spice Infused Bitters

1. Combine all of the ingredients in a mixing glass with ice, stir, and strain into the coupe.

2. Garnish with the expressed orange peel and Maraschino cherry.

DIOSA VERDE

Angelenos love both a good green juice and tequila. Why not both at once?

GLASSWARE: Rocks glass rimmed with spicy sugar
GARNISH: Lime wedge

- 2 oz. Lobos 1701 Tequila
- 1 oz. fresh lime juice
- ¾ oz. grilled tomatillo juice
- ¼ oz. grilled nopales juice
- ½ oz. agave syrup

1. Combine all of the ingredients in a cocktail shaker with ice, shake well, and strain into the prepared rocks glass over ice.

2. Garnish with the lime wedge.

HORCHATA PAINKILLER

CANOPY CLUB

Head to the roof of the Shay Hotel in Culver City to sip tropical cocktails poolside at the Canopy Club. It's a great spot any time of day, but sunsets always look better several stories up with a drink in your hand.

GLASSWARE: Collins glass

GARNISH: Pineapple wedge and pineapple leaf

- 1½ oz. reposado tequila
- ½ oz. pineapple rum
- ¼ oz. Licor 43
- 2 oz. pineapple juice
- 1 oz. orange juice
- 1 oz. coconut horchata
- 2 dashes Angostura Bitters
- Blue Curaçao, to top

1. Combine all of the ingredients, except the Blue Curaçao, in a cocktail shaker with ice, shake well, and strain into the Collins class over ice.

2. Garnish with the pineapple wedge and pineapple leaf, and top with a few dashes of Blue Curaçao.

CHICLE POP

GLASSWARE: Rocks glass rimmed with salt
GARNISH: Lime wheel

- 1 basil leaf, torn in half
- 2 oz. tequila blanco
- ¼ oz. prickly pear juice
- 1 oz. watermelon syrup
- 1 oz. fresh lime juice

1. Combine all of the ingredients in a cocktail shaker with ice, shake well, and strain into the prepared rocks glass over ice.

2. Garnish with the lime wheel.

CHAMP'S MARGARITA

CHAMP CITY BAR AND LOUNGE

Champ City opened right before the world shut down in March 2020. To say it's been a bumpy road for this restaurant and bar is an understatement. But thanks to new ownership, renovations, and new menus, including a drinks program created by Rooterfish's Julian Garroway Jr. and longtime local bartender Robert Bahena, the future is looking bright. This is a great place to stop before or after a Rams or Chargers game at SoFi Stadium.

GLASSWARE: Tajín-rimmed tumbler

- **4 oz. tequila**
- **1 splash agave**
- **2 oz. sweet & sour mix**

1. Combine all of the ingredients in a cocktail shaker with ice, shake well, and strain into the prepared tumbler.

LOS ANGELES COCKTAILS — 209

TEQUILA SMASH

CHAMP CITY BAR AND LOUNGE

E asy to make, even easier to drink—enjoying a cocktail doesn't need to be hard.

◇✦◇

GLASSWARE: Tumbler

GARNISH: Lemon wedge

- 4 oz. tequila
- 2 oz. pineapple juice
- 2 oz. cranberry juice
- 1 splash grenadine

1. Combine all of the ingredients in a cocktail shaker with ice, shake well, and strain into the tumbler over ice.

THE VALLEY

OY BAR

THE GREEN ROOM

Part of the San Fernando Valley, aka the Valley, is in Los Angeles, but even the parts that aren't still hold on to the city's overall spirit.

DOCTOR'S AWAY

People in the know describe Oy Bar as a dive bar because the place is dimly lit and the regulars are true locals. But those same people also know that the elevated bar food menu goes above and beyond, and that if you want more than a cold beer or a well drink, the cocktail menu provides plenty of interesting options. Now you know.

GLASSWARE: Rocks glass

GARNISH: Orange oils, dehydrated apple chip

- **2 oz. Old Grand-Dad Bonded Bourbon**
- **1 bar spoon Baking Spice– Infused Le Père Jules Pommeau de Normandie**
- **1 bar spoon rich demerara syrup (2:1)**
- **2 dashes House Aromatic Bitters**

1. Combine all of the ingredients in the rocks glass. Stir over a big rock of ice.

2. Garnish with the orange oils and dehydrated apple chip.

BAKING SPICE-INFUSED POMMEAU DE NORMANDIE: In a saucepan over medium heat, toast 2 cinnamon sticks, 1 tbsp. cardamom, and 1 tsp. allspice berries for 7 to 10 minutes, constantly stirring to avoid burning. Add 1 bottle (750ml) Le Père Jules Pommeau de Normandie to the toasted spices, bring to a boil, and then reduce heat and simmer for 20 minutes. Allow to cool 1 hour before straining and storing.

HOUSE AROMATIC BITTERS: Combine 2 parts Angostura Bitters with 1 part Bittermens Transatlantic Bitters.

SIXTH HOUR

OY BAR

T his drink is sure to brighten the dreariest of days.

GLASSWARE: Nick and Nora glass

- 1 oz. La Luna Mezcal Cupreata
- ½ oz. Paranubes Oaxacan Rum
- ¾ oz. fresh lime juice
- ¾ oz. Grapefruit Cordial
- 1 dash House Aromatic Bitters (see page 217)

1. Combine all of the ingredients in a cocktail shaker with ice, shake well, and fine-strain into the Nick and Nora glass.

GRAPEFRUIT CORDIAL: Zest 4 grapefruits, 2 lemons, and 1 lime and set the zest aside. Juice all of the zested fruit and fine-strain. Combine the juice with 1.25 parts granulated sugar and whisk to integrate. Once the sugar is dissolved, add the zest, 1 tsp. salt, and 1 tsp. fennel. Place the cordial in an immersion bath for 4 hours at 135°F and then place it in an ice bath for 15 minutes. Strain and store.

THREE WISHES

This rooftop bar in Burbank offers expansive views and wonderful drinks. The bar's design is inspired by the "green rooms" where celebs and other Hollywood folk relax before and after shows and appearances, which explains why the menu draws from popular movies, ranging from *Grease* to *Fight Club*, and, in the case of Three Wishes, *Aladdin*.

GLASSWARE: Teacups

GARNISH: Bachelor buttons

- 2 oz. jasmine tea
- 2 oz. honey
- 3 red seedless grapes
- 1 oz. fresh lemon juice
- 1 oz. red wine
- 4 oz. Monkey 47 Schwarzwald Dry Gin
- Dry ice

1. Infuse the jasmine tea in hot water.

2. Combine 2 oz. steeped tea with the honey and stir to create a syrup.

3. Muddle the grapes in a cocktail shaker, then pour in the tea mixture, lemon juice, and red wine. Dry shake.

4. In a second shaker, combine the gin with ice, shake well, and pour into the teacups over a single large ice cube.

5. Add dry ice to a tea infuser and place that in a teapot. Add the muddled mixture, which will create "smoke." Pour the teapot mixture into the mugs to fill. Garnish with a bachelor button.

ABOUT THE AUTHORS

Kimberly Zerkel is a freelance writer. After a decade of living and teaching in Paris, she returned to the United States to live in San Francisco, California. She has regularly contributed to the *San Francisco Chronicle* and *Represent Collaborative*, among other publications. Kimberly currently resides in Joplin, Missouri.

Joseph D. Solis is a hospitality and wine and spirits expert known for his luxury approach to cocktails and experiences. In addition to being a cocktail atelier, Joseph is CEO and founder of Sol Hospitality Group, a LA- and NYC-based boutique agency that creates "liquid to lips" experiences. Clients include Moët Hennessy, Diageo, Bacardi, William Grant & Sons, and brands such as Hennessy, Ciroc Vodka, DeLeon Tequila, D'ussé, Tanqueray, and Belvedere Vodka, as well as numerous luxury private clients from around the world.

PHOTOGRAPHY CREDITS

Pages 10, 11, 14, 21, 22, 30, 32, 33, courtesy of Library of Congress.

Pages 1, 3, 4, 5, 6, 19, 27, 33, 34, 46, 47, 58, 59, 71, 72, 102, 104, 105, 158, 159, 192, 193, 210, 211, 222, 224, 226, 238 used under official license from Shutterstock.com.

All other images used courtesy of the respective bars and restaurants.

INDEX

—About Cider Mill Press Book Publishers—

Good ideas ripen with time. From seed to harvest, Cider Mill Press brings fine reading, information, and entertainment together between the covers of its creatively crafted books. Our Cider Mill bears fruit twice a year, publishing a new crop of titles each spring and fall.

"Where Good Books Are Ready for Press"

501 Nelson Place
Nashville, Tennessee 37214

cidermillpress.com